THE RETURN OF THE OLD GODS

MY OCCULT JOURNEY
ON THE PAGAN PATH

CHRISTOPHER McINTOSH

Inner Traditions
Rochester, Vermont

Inner Traditions
One Park Street
Rochester, Vermont 05767
www.InnerTraditions.com

Text stock is SFI certified

Cataloging-in-Publication Data for this title is available from the Library of Congress

ISBN 979-8-88850-093-4 (print)
ISBN 979-8-88850-094-1 (ebook)

Printed and bound in the United States by Lake Book Manufacturing, LLC
The text stock is SFI certified. The Sustainable Forestry Initiative® program
promotes sustainable forest management.

10 9 8 7 6 5 4 3 2 1

Text design by Priscilla Harris Baker and layout by Debbie Glogover
This book was typeset in Garamond Premier Pro with Alverata, Frutiger LT Std,
and Thrillers used as display typefaces

To send correspondence to the author of this book, mail a first-class letter
to the author c/o Inner Traditions • Bear & Company, One Park Street,
Rochester, VT 05767, and we will forward the communication, or contact the
author directly via Facebook Messenger.

Scan the QR code and save 25% at InnerTraditions.com.
Browse over 2,000 titles on spirituality, the occult, ancient
mysteries, new science, holistic health, and natural medicine.

THE CALL
OF THE
OLD GODS

"Throughout his multiple careers in diplomacy, academia, and publishing, Christopher has never lost sight of higher realities. His many books celebrate the companions of this vision: Rosicrucians, astrologers, monarchs and magi, occultists and creators—like himself—of symbolic gardens honoring the old gods of Europe. They now culminate in one of the great spiritual autobiographies and a paragon of the soul's navigation through the troubled waters of modernity."

JOSCELYN GODWIN, PROFESSOR EMERITUS AT COLGATE UNIVERSITY
AND AUTHOR OF *THE PAGAN DREAM OF THE RENAISSANCE*
AND *ATLANTIS AND THE CYCLES OF TIME*

"Part spiritual autobiography, part exploration of ancient and contemporary pagan spirituality, this vivid and intensely personal memoir by one of the most respected esotericists of our time is required reading for anyone interested in today's lively renewal of polytheistic faiths."

JOHN MICHAEL GREER, AUTHOR OF
THE TWILIGHT OF PLUTO AND *THE KING IN ORANGE*

"Christopher McIntosh is the Forrest Gump of the esoteric world. With Taoist, almost magical abilities, he has been everywhere and met everyone in the 60+ years he has traversed the field of arcane studies. His fascinating autobiography is not only a documentation of his personal path and studies but also a riveting account of how he and a handful of others have transformed and rehabilitated the esoteric field. Endlessly fascinating!"

HILMAR ÖRN HILMARSSON, COMPOSER, MUSICIAN,
AND HIGH PRIEST OF THE ÁSATRÚ ASSOCIATION IN ICELAND

"Written by a highly respected member of the occult and heathen community, *The Call of the Old Gods* is an inspiring narrative showing how paganism is not a relic of a bygone era but has a meaningful place in our modern world. It also has a much broader social message, for the encounters, spiritual conflicts, revelations, and practices the author describes are those that all free-spirited seekers of deeper truth must engage with on their own individual paths."

RICHARD RUDGLEY, AUTHOR OF *THE RETURN OF ODIN*

"The path of Christopher McIntosh's rich and varied life meandered over and under the threads of Wyrd. His journeys through numerous countries and countless terrains created a tapestry of varied textures and hues, some gentle, some intense. In this deeply personal memoir Christopher connects the dots. He has been truly called by the old gods."

INGRID KINCAID, AUTHOR OF *LOST TEACHINGS OF THE RUNES*

"Christopher McIntosh's eighty-year journey on the pagan path offers enthralling insights by a master storyteller. To read this book is to take that journey, to share his magical moments and beautiful rituals, and to experience the profoundly re-enchanting powers of the pagan revival. This book will change the way you see and feel our world. Io Pan!"

LIONEL SNELL (ALIAS RAMSEY DUKES), AUTHOR OF
S.S.O.T.B.M.E.: AN ESSAY ON MAGIC

"In an age when science now recognizes the widespread role of intelligence and intention in many living species, McIntosh's gentle, humorous, yet respectful pagan path makes perfect sense. The old gods are renamed and rediscovered, and this very personal and original book is a start to taking a look at those millennia of practical communication with natural spirits."

FREDERICK TURNER, FOUNDERS PROFESSOR EMERITUS,
THE BASS SCHOOL OF ARTS, HUMANITIES AND TECHNOLOGY
AT THE UNIVERSITY OF TEXAS AT DALLAS

"In *The Call of the Old Gods*, renowned author Christopher McIntosh invites us on a unique journey through the occult of the twentieth and twenty-first centuries, featuring many remarkable people and places, as he shares his distinctive path rediscovering the gods and ways of ancient Europe."

ARTHUR VERSLUIS, AUTHOR OF
THE SECRET HISTORY OF WESTERN SEXUAL MYSTICISM

To my wife, Donate, and to my sons, Angus and Jason,

and my grandchildren, Daniel, Abigail, Leo, and John,

with love, and to the memory of my dear parents,

Angus and Barbara.

Heathen, *n. A benighted creature who has the folly to worship something that he can see and feel.*

AMBROSE BIERCE,
THE DEVIL'S DICTIONARY

Contents

PREFACE

A Spiral Journey

The journey of my life has been a spiral one. Unlike those lives that proceed in a straight line toward some preconceived goal, mine has been more like a journey through a maze in which the path twists back and forth, taking false turns and coming to dead ends, but gradually spiraling toward the center. Alternatively, I sometimes think of my life as the voyage of a sailor who has traveled to many distant places and finally come to rest in a safe harbor.

I describe my path as "pagan," but I also use the word "heathen." Just to clarify these terms, I use "pagan" as an umbrella term for all polytheistic, nature-oriented religions and their modern revivals. Although the word "heathen" is sometimes treated as a synonym for "pagan," it is generally used in this book to refer to a subcategory of paganism, namely the Nordic tradition.

Acknowledgments

It is customary at the beginning of a book to include a thank-you list of names. In this case there are so many names to mention that they would practically fill a book of their own, but one I must single out, namely my wife, Donate, for her loving encouragement, advice, and feedback, support through the difficult patches, and careful checking of the book for errors and omissions. Warmest thanks go to many others who have played a part in the story of my life: my family, close and extended; my loved ones; my friends from childhood onward; my mentors of various kinds including certain teachers, writers, artists, and thinkers; my fellow seekers on the great path; those who provided help, material, or information for this book; and, last but not least, all at Inner Traditions involved in the commissioning, editing, production, sales, and promotion of the book. A big thank-you to you all.

PROLOGUE

A Spiritual Homecoming

The scene is a sacred grove of birch trees in a secluded spot amid the flat countryside of Lower Saxony, north Germany, on a midwinter evening. As twilight descends a small group of a dozen or so—men, women, and children, myself included—process along a path lined with storm lanterns, take our places within the grove, and form a circle around a ring of stones within which a log fire waits to be lit. We are here to celebrate the winter solstice according to Asatru, the way of those who honor the old gods of northern Europe.

One of the group circumambulates the ritual space, raising a wooden Hammer of Thor at each of the four compass points and in the center and calling upon the spirits of each one to hallow our circle and keep watch. Then it is time for me to play my part. I step forward with a flaming torch and set the fire alight, reciting in German: "In the name of the High Gods I light this sacred fire of purification and creation. Let flame upon flame blaze forth so that life, light, and warmth may increase and not be extinguished before their time."

As the fire comes to life we all sing a familiar song called the "Song of a Thousand Gods." Then the ritual proceeds with a speech honoring Baldur, the god of light, who is killed through the cunning

1

of Loki, god of mischief, but is reborn every year at midwinter. There are more songs. A mead horn circulates three times—once for the gods, once for the ancestors, and once for anything else we may wish to speak about. Each of us drinks from the horn and speaks a toast or some thoughtful, heartfelt words.

I look round at the cheerful faces glowing in the firelight. I am warmed in body by its glow and in my heart by the presence of kindred spirits reaching out to each other in a shared ritual, lovingly performed. I am home. It has been a long journey.

1

A Hermetic Baptism

My earliest memories, which reach back to the age of three, are of Oxford, where my father taught English at the college of Christ Church. They are memories of an idyll: hushed college quadrangles, sunlit gardens sequestered behind old stone walls, the swish of oars on the Cherwell River, the deer in Magdalen park, my father building a snowman in the garden of our house in Norham Road, my mother dressing my newborn brother, David. In the main quadrangle of Christ Church there is a fountain with a statue of Mercury (or Hermes, to use his Greek name) and goldfish swimming in the water. One day, peering at the goldfish, I lost my balance, fell into the water, and had to be fished out by my father. Later, when I became fascinated by things Hermetic, I came to look back on that event as my Hermetic baptism. On another occasion I fell into the river and could easily have drowned if someone hadn't pulled me out. I wasn't afraid, just fascinated by the greenish water surrounding me and the bubbles rising to the sunlit surface. I also remember the sound of bells, the great bell of Christ Church (called Tom) and many other bells, whose tolling seemed to slow rather than hasten the passage of time. The untarnished idyll of Oxford and the England of my early

3

Fig. 1.1. Myself, aged one and a quarter, drawn by my father.

CHRISTOPHER

DECEMBER '44.

A.M.

childhood have stayed with me over the years and perhaps explain my later fascination with the never-never lands of fable and fiction—Agartha, Shambhala, Shangri-La, and the Russian Land of the White Waters.

My father's forebears came from Sutherland in the far north of Scotland. One of them, my great-grandfather, was a ship's engineer who settled in the north of England, and my father Angus grew up in Cleadon, County Durham. My grandfather and grandmother were of modest means but wonderful, warmhearted people with a strong appreciation for learning. My father, who was educated at state schools, proved to be a brilliant pupil and in due course won a scholarship to Oriel College, Oxford. After taking a first in English he went on a scholarship to do graduate work in philology at Harvard University. There he befriended a fellow student called John Bainbridge and fell in love with his sister Barbara. The family had a farm in Connecticut and an apartment on fashionable Gramercy

Park in New York City. My mother's father was a prominent surgeon and, among other things, a pioneer in the treatment of cancer. My parents were married in 1939 at the family home in Connecticut by the famous preacher and author Norman Vincent Peale, and my father took his bride back to England just in time for the start of the Second World War, most of which he spent as part of the decoding team at Bletchley Park, while my mother also did wartime work at nearby Woburn Abbey.

I was born on September 21, 1943, in the village of Pembury, near Tunbridge Wells, Kent, to which my mother had been evacuated for the delivery, presumably because it was considered safer from bombardment. The date of my birth is significant, because my parents later told me that they had delayed conceiving a child until they could be sure that the Allies would win the war. The event that convinced them must have been the German defeat at Stalingrad in December 1942, exactly nine months before my birth. I have often thought about this fact and wondered if, according to the theory of reincarnation, the soul of some German victim of Stalingrad had become reborn in Pembury, Kent. This might account for the intense love of Germany that I later developed. I should add that not long ago I mentioned these thoughts to a clairvoyant friend of mine, who went into a brief trance and then said that the Stalingrad part was true, but that I was a Russian and not a German soldier. This also made partial sense to me, as I have long had a great love of Russia as well as Germany.

But does reincarnation really happen? If so, I would have to decide between the German and the Russian, as it seems unlikely that two people could reincarnate in one body at the same time. Furthermore, unless one were born again within the same family, one would acquire a whole new set of ancestors with every reincarnation. I found this idea hard to accept. On the other hand, why do certain people from the past, ancestors or not, seem to call out to me? I believe the answer lies in a concept that I would call "ancestors in spirit." These may at the same time be blood ancestors, or they may be completely unrelated. How these ancestries in spirit come about is a great mystery. My former wife Katherine told me that, when she visited Israel, despite her Jewish ancestry she felt no sense of ancestral roots there, whereas on her first trip to India, when she disembarked from the plane and mingled with the bustling crowd in the Delhi airport, she had a feeling of homecoming that almost made her cry. Somehow on the etheric plane a connection had been established between her and the spirit of India. And similarly, perhaps those two soldiers, in the moment of dying at Stalingrad, for some reason reached out in spirit to a newborn child in Kent, England.

As for my own blood ancestors, I have the benefit of two family genealogies, one compiled by my father's mother, Mary McIntosh, the other commissioned by my maternal grandfather, Dr. William Seaman Bainbridge, who was a distinguished surgeon in New York City. The name Seaman was his mother's maiden name, and the chapter on the Seaman pedigree states that the name "can be traced back to the Old Norse personal name of Sigmundr, meaning 'holder of victory.'"

The passage goes on:

> It was a name common to both the early Scandinavians and Germans and appears in England in the Domesday Survey, made by William the Conqueror in 1086. . . . It is held that the name entered England before the year 1000 and was probably originally borne by Viking settlers.[1]

When I read this passage and saw the name Sigmundr, it struck a powerful chord in me and gave me the feeling that here was a blood ancestor who was also one in spirit. I sometimes wonder if it was he who gave me the first push on my journey back to the gods of his people.

Through my maternal grandmother I had some colorful American ancestors. Her father, Thomas Heber Wheeler, grew up in Maine and, as a young man, fell in love with a local girl named Ellen, but was told by her father that he would have to establish himself in the world before he could marry her. It was the 1850s and the time of the California gold rush, so he headed west—a difficult journey, first by ship to the Isthmus of Panama, then across the isthmus by mule, then up to San Francisco on another ship. In San Francisco he lodged with a middle-aged woman he had met on the journey, who owned an establishment that masqueraded as a shirt factory but was in fact a brothel. Evidently the proprietress kept the "seamstresses" away from him.

From there he went up into the hills with a fellow gold-seeker and began prospecting. One day his partner was murdered by robbers, who were quickly apprehended and jailed. Fearing that they might be released on some legal technicality, Thomas and a group of friends made an unsuccessful attempt to break into the jail and lynch the murderers. He was knocked unconscious when a prison guard struck him on the back of his head with the butt of a pistol, and he had a bump on the back of his head for the rest of his life. He then went to work in a gold mine. At the end of one shift he volunteered to go back down and bring up a load of gold at the risk of being asphyxiated by poison gas, which had seeped out into the mine shaft. As a reward he was given a bag of gold dust worth four thousand dollars—a considerable fortune in those days—enabling him to go back east and marry his sweetheart, who was just short of her sixteenth birthday at the time. During my own visits to San Francisco I have often thought of him and may even have retraced his footsteps.

But to return to my own life story—in 1948 the Oxford idyll came to an end and we moved to Edinburgh, where my father had been appointed to the Professorship of English Language and General Linguistics. I believe he was the youngest incumbent in the

Fig. 1.2. Silhouette of the author, made in Edinburgh, c. 1949.

history of the chair. He had a brilliant career ahead of him and was to become a world-renowned expert on Old and Middle English. For me the transition to life in Edinburgh was difficult. The city seemed gray and rather somber after the mellowness of Oxford, and at first I found the Scottish accent harsh and difficult to understand.

Worst of all was the preparatory school to which I was sent at the age of about seven or eight after a phase at a nursery school. The headmaster was an elderly man whom I shall call Pritchard (I withhold his real name out of consideration for his descendants), a scrawny, stooping, shuffling figure with pale, watery eyes and a military moustache. The school was divided into "houses," named after First World War "heroes" like General Haig, General Kitchener, and Admiral Beatty. I was placed in a house named after Haig, one of the most criminally incompetent generals in history, as I later found out. Like many twisted people Pritchard could appear quite avuncular and benevolent. To parents he seemed a reassuring combination of jollity and old-fashioned firmness. In fact he was a sadist of the worst kind—the kind who finds a moral excuse for his sadism. His favored instrument of punishment was a leather slipper, which he kept in a pile of old newspapers in his study. I must have been about eight or nine years old when I was summoned by him one afternoon—for what offense I had no idea—and made to drop my trousers and bend

Fig. 1.3. With my brother, David (*left*), in front
of our house in Edinburgh in the early 1950s,
wearing our prep school uniforms.
The picture was taken by our mother.

over a chair. When Pritchard hit me with the slipper the pain was so intense that I urinated on the chair. In that moment all my childhood innocence and trust was lost. I became taciturn and distrustful of the entire adult world.

Thus my early education, which should have been a wonderful journey of discovery, became a torment. For about five years I endured the school in a state of frozen anxiety, constantly dreading the next beating. During the classes I sat tongue-tied and withdrawn, so that eventually the headmaster became infuriated by my unresponsiveness and had the effrontery to complain to my parents. They, instead of looking for the real cause of the problem, thought there might be something wrong with me and sent me to be examined by a psychiatrist friend of theirs. He too completely misread the situation. Instead of asking himself whether I might be traumatized, he just tested my intelligence, which turned out to be normal, as he reported back to my parents. They were reassured, so nothing changed and the torment of the school went on. You may ask why I didn't speak out. I did and so did my brother, although perhaps not strongly enough, but our parents evidently did not think there was anything untoward about the school. My mother was a sweet woman with a bright, radiant personality and an intelligent mind, but she had a kind of innocent naïveté and was completely deceived by Pritchard's jolly, avuncular manner. As for my father, I think he disliked having to deal with such problems and preferred to ignore them. Later I think he felt very guilty about the whole episode because I remember him once saying gloomily that he preferred not to talk about it.

One tragic consequence of this experience was that emotionally I became intensely withdrawn, almost autistic, which must have been a source of great sadness to my parents. When I lived in New York in the 1990s a highly perceptive woman psychotherapist told me: "When you are angry you get parsimonious with your emotions." She was spot on. I did become parsimonious with my emotions—not only with my parents but with many other people as well—when an outburst of rage would have been much healthier. In time I buried the whole episode and became outwardly a relatively normal individual, but inwardly there remained much damage that would take decades to repair.

Our family home was a lovely early-nineteenth-century house in Blacket Place, a secluded enclave of such houses in the south of Edinburgh. Later we also had a country cottage near Gifford, about an hour's drive from the city. The household consisted of my parents, my brother David, my sister June (born in 1956), and my American maternal grandmother June, who came to live with us around the early 1950s. In character my brother, David, was always very different from myself. He was and remains outgoing, gregarious, always giving of his warm, extroverted personality, whereas I have continued to be somewhat introverted and reserved. He is practical and worldly, while I am otherworldly and a dreamer. Despite, or perhaps because of, these differences, there has come to be a deep bond of affection and mutual respect between us. As for my sister June, the thirteen years between us meant that for the most crucial years of her adolescence I was already away in England earning a living and raising a family, and it was only later, when she was grown up and we were both living in London for a time, that we developed the kind of familial closeness that siblings should have.

Thanks to my grandmother's money there were various domestic staff. There was Miss Cockburn, who was nanny to David and me and then to June, our live-in cook Miss Gardner, and various household helpers of whom the longest serving was Mrs. Cox. There were also other helpers who came and went over the years. One I remember particularly was Lily Millar, who later became something of a celebrity. A strong personality, she was sometimes heartwarming and entertaining, at other times harsh and bossy. She had grown up in a bitterly poor family in the Scottish border town of Duns under circumstances that would have crushed a weaker person, but she had a will of steel and a determination to make something of her life. At the time she came to us she had a failed marriage behind her and two sons. There followed another marriage, another son, and another divorce, then many years later she married the heir to the Earldom of Galloway, and when he succeeded to the title she became the Countess of Galloway and a famous and colorful figure in the Edinburgh social scene. Her remarkable story is told in Louise Carpenter's book *An Unlikely Countess* (published in 2004).

Fig. 1.4. Our house in Blacket Place, Edinburgh.
PHOTOGRAPH BY THE AUTHOR

Fig. 1.5. My parents in front of their country cottage
at Gifford, East Lothian, in 1986.

PHOTOGRAPH BY THE AUTHOR

One bright spot in my early childhood was our au pair, Ingrid Koch, a German student whom my parents had welcomed into their home in a spirit of reconciliation toward her country. For my schoolmates and friends on the block, when they played their silly war games, the Germans were still the enemy, but not for me. I adored Ingrid, so how could I not like her country? She was like a fairy godmother to me. Everything about her, even down to the way she had arranged her room, breathed a subtle refinement and serenity and the kind of foreignness that I found immensely appealing. From Ingrid I learned my first words of German and she planted the seed of my love for her homeland. I remained in touch with her to her death in 2021, and it is partly thanks to her that I have made Germany my home.

Fig. 1.6. My German "fairy godmother,"
Ingrid Pickhardt, née Koch, at her home in
Bad Honnef, circa 1983.

PHOTOGRAPH BY THE AUTHOR

Our neighbors in Blacket Place included some prominent people, such as the world-famous geneticist C. H. Waddington and the musicologist Hans Gal, a Jewish émigré from Austria, who was a leading expert on Wagner—how much I could have learned from him if I had known that I would later become a devoted Wagnerite, but that lay far in the future.

For most of my early life my bedroom had a view of Arthur's Seat, the lion-shaped mountain that towers oddly over the southeastern side of the city. Perhaps there was some synchronicity involved there, because I loved the stories about King Arthur and the Knights of the Round Table. In fact I was fascinated by the whole world of

legends and fairy tales and avidly read anything in that area that I
could get hold of. It was symptomatic of the dreamy, romantic streak
in my nature, which has never left me. That was probably one of
the things that helped to keep me sane during the dismal years at
Pritchard's school.

At the age of thirteen I moved to the Edinburgh Academy, an
old-established school with rather austere, gray-stone buildings located
in Henderson Row in the New Town. For my first term my awkward-
ness made me unpopular with my classmates, but gradually I settled in
and began to make friends. I still had my distrust of the adult world,
which included most of the masters, but there were a few whom I
respected. One was the strict but genial Latin teacher Mr. McEwan,
a Kiplingesque figure who had been in the Indian Civil Service and
looked the part with his military moustache, tweed suit, and watch
chain. On occasions he even wore a monocle. Another I liked was the
German teacher, Mr. Head, a kindly, mild-mannered Welshman with
a deep love of the German classics, which he skillfully imparted to his
pupils. And there was Mr. Johnson-Jones, the French teacher, urbane,
dapper, and cosmopolitan, with whom I later established a personal
friendship. As for sports, I was never any good at team games like
rugby and cricket, but I took enthusiastically to squash, tennis, and
especially golf, which has remained a passion of mine to this day. On
the serene fairways and greens of the golf course I felt free and my
spirit could breathe and expand. In those days golf was not the expensive sport that it has now become, with impossibly crowded courses
and long waiting lists for club membership. I was a member of a club
within a few minutes' walk of our house and had the pick of any
number of excellent courses in and around the city.

The Edinburgh Academy regularly organized trips abroad, and
I took part in two of them—one to Paris in 1957 and the second
to Rome and Florence the following year. In Rome we attended a
public audience with Pope Pius XII in St. Peter's Basilica. I don't

Fig. 1.7. Myself (*left*), aged fourteen, on the roof of
the Duomo, Florence, with Peter McLeod (*center*) and
David McDougall (*right*), on a school trip to Italy in 1958.
PHOTOGRAPH FROM THE AUTHOR'S COLLECTION

remember being particularly overawed by the pomp and the impos-
ing surroundings, nor by the Pope, himself, as he was carried on a
throne, shoulder-high, through the crowd filling the nave. What
impressed me much more was something I saw in the Uffizi Gallery
in Florence, namely Botticelli's painting *Primavera* with its distinctly
pagan theme. I admit that, from the perspective of my present self
and worldview, I may be succumbing to a temptation to look back
and join certain dots in my life that seem to lead inexorably to where
I am now in my spiritual development. Had I ended up as, say, a
Marxist, I might be joining up a different set of dots. And perhaps

there is a sense in which we actually shape our own past retrospectively according to which set of dots we join.

At any rate, when I stood in front of Botticelli's painting I was spellbound. I knew very little about classical mythology and had no idea who the figures in the painting were: Venus, her son Amor with bow and arrow, the three Graces, Mercury, Flora, and the nymph Chloris being chased by Zephyros, the west wind. The scene was set in a shady orange grove, the lush fruit glowing against the dark branches, and the ground was covered with flowers and mushrooms (was the artist perhaps in a psychedelic trance when he painted the picture?). It may have been precisely because of my ignorance and inability to analyze the painting that it spoke to me so directly and vividly. In retrospect I think this was my first encounter with the classical pagan gods in all their sensual, life-affirming vitality. Had I realized this at the time it might have had a life-transforming effect on me, but I was not yet ready to be transformed. I stood mesmerized for a few moments and then moved on. But I believe some kind of seed had been planted, which was to germinate much later.

Meanwhile I continued for a time to regard myself more or less as a Christian. My parents both came from Nonconformist backgrounds—my father Methodist and my mother Baptist—and they had not had me baptized as an infant, preferring to let me decide later for myself one way or the other. I don't remember deciding deliberately against baptism. I just never expressed a wish to be baptized, and nobody pressed me, but up to the age of sixteen I was a believing Christian. My mother had a very sincere faith, and said a prayer at my bedside every evening until I was about ten or eleven. My father was a Christian in his own way, although he didn't talk very much about it, and he often came with us to church. We worshipped at a Presbyterian church, picturesquely located on the shore of Duddingston Loch by Arthur's Seat. I don't recall any sudden disenchantment with Christianity—I just gradually ceased to feel a connection with it. The age of sixteen found me pretty much an agnostic, but deep down I must have had some dimly felt spiritual need because I somehow became interested in Buddhism and attempted to start a Buddhist society at the school—the "Buddhist League" as I called it—which collapsed after only one meeting.

Thinking about that episode it strikes me how limited the possibilities were at that time for someone looking for some form of alternative spirituality outside Christianity. There was Theosophy, which at that time was unknown to me. There was also Rudolf Steiner's Anthroposophy. I had heard of Steiner in connection with the Waldorf schools, but had no idea what his teaching was. Of movements like Thelema, the Gurdjieff work, and Gardner's Wicca I was completely ignorant. How could I know about them when there was as yet no New Age scene and very few esoteric bookshops and magazines? I often think how different my adolescent years would have been if I had become a Pagan at that age. But the only alternative that I was aware of was Buddhism, about which there was a degree of cultural awareness thanks to writers on the subject like Christmas Humphreys. So for a short period I called myself a Buddhist.

In due course I wrote the episode off as a piece of youthful folly and reverted partially to a positivist and rationalist position. At the same time I remained fascinated by the strange and bizarre. I loved the exquisitely decadent art of Aubrey Beardsley and the weird images of the surrealists. My literary tastes also reflected the dichotomy in me. I avidly read Orwell's *Nineteen Eighty-Four* and Huxley's *Brave New World*, but also Bram Stoker's *Dracula* and Mary Shelley's *Frankenstein*. Later I became fascinated by the perversely brilliant works of William Burroughs after hearing a recording of him reading from *The Naked Lunch* in his strangely hypnotic, droning, nasal voice. I began to write things myself—short stories, poems, and short-lived attempts at novels. I also painted a lot—landscapes, abstract shapes, and some crude surrealistic efforts. My fondness for surrealists like Dalí was part of my penchant for the weird and bizarre.

Edinburgh became a vibrant place to be. There were coffee bars where you could listen to poetry readings or live jazz. There was the Paperback Bookshop in George Square, run by a genial, hippie-like American called Jim Haynes, which was a rendezvous for the avant-garde scene in Edinburgh. There were also intriguing antiquarian bookshops where you could find treasures for almost nothing. Above all there was the Edinburgh Festival in late August and early September, which brought an embarras de richesses of plays, concerts, and exhibitions.

I had a congenial circle of friends, three in particular who were school contemporaries: David, Iain, and Douglas. Iain, a deeply thoughtful, rather withdrawn person, shared my love of the German language and many of my out-of-the-way literary tastes. I subsequently fell out of touch with these friends, but they came back into my life after some decades in an unexpected way, of which more will be discussed later. I went out with a succession of girls, some of them au pairs in the neighborhood, although I was not yet sexually active, and the transition to an adult sexual life was to prove extremely difficult for me. Still, on the whole in those late teenage years life was exciting, fun, and full of possibility, but there were some testing times ahead and a long way to go on the spiritual quest.

2

Magic and Mystery in Oxford and London

Throughout my school days it had been my dream to return to Oxford as an undergraduate, and in the winter of 1961 I went down to take the entrance exam for Christ Church ("Candidates will answer all of Section A and one question each from Sections B and C"). The exam was held in the magnificent Great Hall that was later used as part of the set for the Harry Potter films. A couple of weeks later I received a letter from the college offering me a place to read philosophy, politics, and economics, beginning the following autumn. In the interval I spent a semester at Columbia University, New York, thanks to the influence of my uncle, John Bainbridge, who was dean of the law school. I sat in on various lectures and took a beginners' course in Russian, which stood me in good stead later on.

In October of 1962 I duly took up my place at Christ Church. Unfortunately, I threw away most of what Oxford had to offer. When I went there I was an outwardly arrogant, inwardly deeply insecure person who didn't know who he was. I performed badly academically and alienated certain of my teachers. Inwardly I was adrift with no firm anchor of belief in anything. But a dormant pagan self must already have been there, buried somewhere deep inside me, because one night, when I was home during a vacation, I had a dream in which I saw the god Pan leading a procession of maenads through a wood while playing his pipe. It might have been prompted by my reading Aleister Crowley's *Hymn to Pan*:

> *Pan, io Pan, come over the sea*
> *From Sicily and from Arcady,*
> *Roaming as Bacchus with fauns and pards*
> *And nymphs and satyrs for thy guards.*[1]

The next day I painted a picture of the vision, which I discovered decades later when clearing out the attic of the Edinburgh house.

Fig. 2.1. An oil painting that I produced at about age twenty-one, following a dream in which I saw Pan leading a procession of maenads. See also color plate 1.

Fig. 2.2. Myself as an Oxford undergraduate in 1963.

PHOTOGRAPH FROM THE AUTHOR'S COLLECTION

Two particularly significant things happened in my life while I was at Oxford. One was that I cofounded a writers' club called—for want of a better name—the Anonymous Society of Writers. Some of the other members included Tim Jeal, the cofounder, now a highly successful biographer and novelist; Frederick Turner, who became a professor of English literature in Texas and a well-known poet and literary scholar; and John Aczel, who later went to the United States and became a leading Scientologist.

Oxford societies had to have a senior member from among the faculty, and ours was J. I. M. Stewart, an English don at Christ Church who wrote detective novels under the name of Michael Innes. We also wanted a couple of prominent names from outside the university as honorary members, so I wrote to William Burroughs in Tangier where he was then living, and he kindly agreed. So did Maurice Girodias, owner of the Olympia Press in Paris, which published a curious mixture of erotica and serious avant-garde works by authors like Burroughs and Samuel Beckett. On a visit to Paris I met Girodias and he took me to lunch in the Latin Quarter. He was a charming, urbane person—part French, part English, part Jewish. Decades later I heard that in old age he had become obsessed with perpetual motion machines and kept on trying to make one in defiance of the laws of physics.

For me, one enormously important thing that came out of the Anonymous Society was that I was introduced to the world of the esoteric. John Aczel was fascinated by astrology and persuaded me to read some books about it, which I did, soon sharing his fascination, casting horoscopes and discussing them with him. At around the same time someone told me about Aleister Crowley, unfairly dubbed the "wickedest man in the world," and I was immediately intrigued. I read John Symonds's biography of Crowley, *The Great Beast*, and some of Crowley's own writing such as *Magick in Theory and Practice*, although I was at first mystified by the latter. I began to scour antiquarian bookshops for esoteric material. Names like Eliphas Lévi and Madame Blavatsky became familiar to me.

Another friend told me about Watkins Bookshop, an esoteric bookshop in Cecil Court, off Charing Cross Road in London, which became a favorite haunt of mine, and still is when I visit London. The business was founded in the 1890s by John M. Watkins and moved to Cecil Court in 1901. Among the early customers were Aleister Crowley, the poet and occultist W. B. Yeats, the Theosophist G. R. S. Mead, and the esoteric scholar and Rosicrucian A. E. Waite. John Watkins's son Geoffrey began working in the shop in 1919, eventually taking it over and running it for many decades. As a regular frequenter of the shop I got to know him quite well and found him to be not only a charming and courteous person but a veritable walking encyclopedia. Mention any subject, however obscure, and he could recommend a book about it and tell you the names of the author and publisher, the dates of various editions, and which edition

Fig. 2.3. Watkins Bookshop, London, in 1975.

PHOTOGRAPH BY THE AUTHOR

was best. He had great generosity and once lent me a rare French manuscript from his private collection while I was working on my book *Eliphas Lévi and the French Occult Revival*. More than a bookshop, Watkins was a meeting-place, a crossroads, a treasure-house of esoteric knowledge.

The other significant thing that happened to me while an undergraduate was that on a visit to Paris during the spring vacation of 1964 I met an English girl called Robin, who was to become my first wife. She was working there as a secretary for an American film company and sharing a flat in the suburbs with a group of other young people. She was bright, lively, attractive, and outgoing. I was badly mixed up. I had buried the trauma of the prep school, but the inner scars were still there. What little sex I had experienced up to then had been clumsy and joyless, and I despaired of ever having a full and satisfying physical relationship. In short, I was at a low ebb psychologically and emotionally, although I concealed it well, and I reached out to her wholesome, vivacious personality. I fell in love with her and she with me. We became engaged that summer during a visit to her family's summer cottage in Fowey, Cornwall, and we were married a year later, having done the old-fashioned thing and postponed sex until after the wedding. We had a Church of England wedding at Ashtead in Surrey, where her parents lived, went off to Ireland for our honeymoon, and came back to a flat in Highgate, London. Almost exactly a year later our elder son, Angus, was born. Our second son, Jason, followed three years after that, by which time we were living at Berkhamsted, Hertfordshire, and I was commuting to work in London.

My first job, while we were still living in London, was with a small publishing firm, Newman Neame, in Fitzroy Square. The firm specialized in company histories, industrial house magazines, and the like. Unfortunately I made a mess of the job and left after a year, but there was one important outcome. The firm published a series of general knowledge booklets called Take Home Books for free distribution in factories, and I wrote one on astrology. I then conceived the idea of expanding the booklet into a general history of astrology. My friend and former Newman Neame colleague John Atkinson had gone to work for the publisher Hutchinson, and he put me in touch with Daniel Brostoff, who ran the esoteric Rider imprint within the Hutchinson group. I submitted a synopsis and some sample text and was duly commissioned to write the book, which came out in 1969 under the main Hutchinson imprint as *The Astrologers and their Creed*.

The foreword to the book was written by Agehananda Bharati (real name Leopold Fischer), an Austrian with an extraordinary background, which he described in his memoir *The Ochre Robe*. Having become fascinated by India, he served on the German side during the Second World War in the Free India Legion of Chandra Bhose and at one point was NCO in charge of an army brothel. After the war he became an itinerant monk in India, then emigrated to the United States where he became a professor of anthropology at Syracuse University. When he came to London Daniel Brostoff invited him, along with John Atkinson and myself, to lunch at Bertorelli, a restaurant on Charlotte Street. He was a portly, genial figure, full of Austrian bonhomie and many amusing anecdotes. Perhaps helped by his name, the book did well, had some good reviews, and later went into French and US editions. It made me feel like a proper author at last, and it was to have important ramifications for the subsequent course of my life. While doing research for the book, I came into contact with other esoteric traditions—alchemy, Kabbalah, Rosicrucianism, Golden Dawn magic. There opened up an exciting world for me to write about, and the time was ripe because there was a growing interest in these subjects—mostly on a popular level, but they were also just beginning to attract the serious attention of certain academics.

Meanwhile Robin's father, Edward Court, who was a senior director of the International Publishing Corporation, which produced a range of magazines, had helped me to get a job as an editorial assistant on one of them, *Country Life*, a weekly magazine covering a unique range of material. There were articles on farming, ornithology, field sports, and gardening, but also on art, architecture, music, travel, and much else. We occupied a beautiful building in Covent Garden, designed for *Country Life* by Edwin Lutyens, and the office I shared with three other members of the editorial staff was like a country house drawing room. I started off as a subeditor, which meant preparing the articles for press. It was pleasant, relatively undemanding work, and the hours were civilized and overtime was rare. After a while I started writing things for the magazine— short book reviews and articles on a whole variety of things ranging from folklore to travel. It was an ideal job to combine with a career as an author. I was within easy reach of the essential libraries for my research. Preeminent was the British Museum with its wonderful domed Reading Room—sadly, the library has since moved to other premises and the domed room has become part of the museum space. There was also the Warburg Institute in Woburn Square, which had a superb esoteric collection, the Theosophical Society Library in Gloucester Place, the library of the Folklore Society at University College, and a number of others. Often I was able to combine visits to these libraries with research work for *Country Life*. The office was also very close to Watkins Bookshop, where I often used to browse during the lunch hour.

Looking back, I feel privileged to have experienced London at that period. For someone with my interests it was a paradise. If one were to make a list of the cities that have been important centers of esotericism, the list would include Prague, Amsterdam, Paris, Berlin, San Francisco, and Los Angeles. All of these cities have been thriving centers of esotericism at various times in history. But, at the time that I am talking about—from the late 1960s to the late '80s, when I worked in London and later moved back there to live—I would argue that London could claim to have been the world capital of esotericism.

There was a sense of continuity with the esoteric traditions of the past, with names from earlier centuries like John Dee, Elias Ashmole, and Francis Barrett and with names from before or just after the Second World War, such as Aleister Crowley, Dion Fortune, A. E. Waite, P. D. Ouspensky, Gerald Gardner, and many others who had been active in and around London. In the 1960s, '70s, and '80s there were many people around who had known or worked with some of these figures. One whom I knew well was Gerald Yorke, scholar and Gloucestershire country squire, who was an advisor to Rider Books and therefore in frequent contact with my friend and editor Daniel Brostoff. Yorke had been Crowley's chief disciple back in the 1930s and had amassed a huge collection of Crowleyana that he had

Fig. 2.4. Gerald Yorke, scholar, esotericist, and country squire at his home in Gloucestershire in the summer of 1982.
PHOTOGRAPH BY THE AUTHOR

deposited at the Warburg Institute. He later turned to Eastern mysticism and edited a number of very important works for publication in the West, including those of the Dalai Lama.

A group of friends and I used to hold a dinner for Yorke once a year at a club near Trafalgar Square, and he would regale us endlessly with very amusing stories about his time with Crowley and about the various occultists and oddballs who came to visit him at his stately home, Forthampton Court. One anecdote concerned Kenneth Anger, the film director and Crowley follower. On an overnight visit to Forthampton Court, Anger asked for permission to cut a magic wand from one of the elm trees on the estate. York mischievously told him that he could do so, provided that he went at dawn in the nude and cut the wand with one stroke of the knife. Next morning at first light Yorke looked out of the window and saw Anger emerging on to a lawn behind the house, throwing off a dressing gown and then walking naked toward an elm tree. Suddenly he leapt in the air with an agonized yell—he had stepped on a dead hedgehog! Undaunted, he walked up to the tree and duly cut his magic wand. Afterward, interpreting the hedgehog as a sign from the gods, he took it home, had it stuffed, and placed it reverently on his mantelpiece.

I also knew people who had worked with Gerald Gardner, founder of the British witchcraft movement or Wicca. Two friends of mine had been in Gardner's coven almost from the very beginning of the movement, which later became so influential all over the world. These people formed an important link between the earlier movements and the newer ones, including those belonging to the whole phenomenon of the New Age, which was just emerging around the late 1960s along with the Hippie movement—the two movements of course overlapped.

Another prominent figure in the esoteric scene of that time was Gareth Knight (real name Basil Wilby), a prolific writer on the Kabbalah, the tarot, ritual magic, and the Western mystery traditions. He had trained in the Society of the Inner Light, founded by Dion Fortune and went on to cofound a correspondence course in Kabbalah, which later became the esoteric order Servants of the Light, later run by Dolores Ashcroft-Nowicki and active in over twenty countries.

Apart from this continuity with the past, London had a certain atmosphere that was conducive to esotericism. It was not as obvious as in some cities. It was partly hidden, and that was part of its attraction. Large areas of London at that time still had a sort of Dickensian quality, which unfortunately has now largely disappeared. It was a feeling that, behind the faintly gray, somber façade of the city, you could expect to make interesting discoveries. You would be walking down some quiet, rather gloomy side street and would come across a book barrow or a dusty bookshop where you would find some esoteric treasure for next to nothing, or you might find some half-crazy prophet holding forth at a street corner. In certain parts of London you had a feeling, rather like in the Philip Pullman trilogy, *His Dark Materials*, that at any moment you could go through an invisible doorway into another world or dimension of reality.

Later, when making intermittent visits to London as an expatriate, I enjoyed visiting old haunts. Many of them were in one particular district, namely Bloomsbury, which has been a kind of nodal point in my life, a sort of railway junction where many exciting journeys have begun. Bloomsbury is rich in esoteric associations and seems to have a way of causing meaningful encounters like the one described by Dion Fortune in her atmospheric novel *The Winged Bull*, which I have before me as I write. It opens on a night of dense fog—what used to be called a "pea souper" in London—when the hero of the story, Murchison, is trying to find his way across the courtyard of the British Museum and suddenly feels impelled to invoke the pagan gods:

> Murchison stood alone in the fog-bound darkness of the fore-court of the British Museum and cried aloud, "Evoe, Iacchus! Io Pan, Pan! Io Pan!"
>
> And echo answered "Io Pan!"
>
> But a voice that was not echo also answered, 'Who is this that invokes the Great God Pan?[2]

Thus begins an encounter that will transform Murchison's life.

I have crossed that forecourt hundreds of times on my way to the British Museum Reading Room, where I did so much research for my books. A stone's throw away in Gordon Square is the German department of Birkbeck College, where I studied part-time for my German degree. And a short distance to the east in Queen Square is the Art Workers' Guild, which for many years was the venue for a series of esoteric conferences, linked with the occult journal *Quest* and run by Marion Green. At the time of writing these are still continuing elsewhere. The first one I attended was around 1969, and I went to many over the years to hear speakers like Gareth Knight, Colin Wilson, and Dolores Ashcroft-Novicki. Marion Green also had a magical ritual group called the Green Circle, which I took part in for a short time in the early 1980s. It was a nostalgic experience for me going back to the Art Workers' Guild again in June 2016 to attend a conference hosted by the Temenos Academy in memory of John Michell, the writer on sacred geography. There was a rich feast of lectures on the general theme of sacred space. Speakers included Arthur Versluis on the magical island of Samothrace, David Fideler on "John Michell and the Landscapes of the Soul," and Tom Bree on the sacred numbers derived from measurements relating to the Earth and the moon.

Afterward there was a dinner for the participants at the Princess Louise pub in High Holborn, a wonderful Victorian pub with an ornate interior, resplendent with colored ceramic tiles, frosted glass, and acres of mahogany paneling—the kind of hostelry that is increasingly rare these days. The decline of the traditional British pub is one of the tragedies that have befallen the country in recent decades. Fortunately the Princess Louise is still there, and so are some fine Bloomsbury pubs like the Museum Tavern, where the nameless Society was launched, and the Plough nearby in Museum Street, where we held our first few meetings.

Perhaps it's more than coincidence that the French nineteenth-century occultist Eliphas Lévi lived in Bloomsbury when he visited London. Walking through the heart of the district, I would have passed his lodgings in Gower Street many times. Halfway down Gower Street you come to Store Street, location of the outstanding esoteric bookshop Treadwell's where in 2012 I gave a lecture on "Eliphas Lévi: Father of Modern Occultism" to promote a

Fig. 2.5. In the Atlantis Bookshop, London, with the owner
Geraldine Beskin, in about 2014, before giving a reading
from my fiction. We are holding my book
Master of the Starlit Grove and Other Stories.

PHOTOGRAPH FROM THE AUTHOR'S COLLECTION

new edition of my book *Eliphas Lévi and the French Occult Revival.*
Among the audience were two people who had been at the original
launch party of the book forty years earlier: my ex-wife Robin, who
had helped me with the research, and Warren Kenton, known for his
books on the Kabbalah under the name of Z'ev ben Shimon Halevi.

Another famous esoteric bookshop in Bloomsbury is the Atlantis
in Museum Street, founded in 1922 and now owned and run by
Geraldine Beskin, a former member of the Society, and her daughter
Bali. To enter it is to cross a threshold into another world. Rather
like a study in Hogwarts school in a Harry Potter film, it combines
otherworldliness with an atmosphere of coziness and warmth. The
shelves are crammed not only with books on everything from astrology to alchemy and from witchcraft to Druidry, but also with tal-

ismans, pentagrams, magic wands, ceremonial daggers, crystal balls, numerous different tarot packs, and statuettes of various gods and goddesses. On the walls in between the bookshelves are portraits of famous people from the world of esotericism such as Aleister Crowley, Madame Blavatsky, and MacGregor Mathers. One of the regular visitors to the shop in its early days was Gerald Gardner, founder of the Wicca movement, who used to hold rituals in the small meeting room in the basement. I have very fond memories of events at the Atlantis, including a reading from my fiction and a launch party for my book *Beyond the North Wind*.

At the other end of Museum Street there used to be another bookshop called Fine Books Oriental, run by my old friend, the late Jeffrey Somers, and his Japanese wife Nobuko. As the name suggested, the shop specialized in books about the Near and Far East. Of Jewish extraction, Jeffrey was a man of many parts and encyclopedic knowledge, who could talk with authority on all sorts of things, including music, the Kabbalah, the Sufis, Japanese new religions, martial arts, and the Gurdjieff work of which he was a leading proponent. He is sorely missed.

Not far away, in an alley off Charing Cross Road, is Watkins Bookshop, which I have already mentioned as being another haunt of mine. It appears, disguised as "Jenkins" bookshop, in my novel *Return of the Tetrad*—one example of the motif of the esoteric bookshop as a literary device. Another typical example is the shop described at the beginning of Edward Bulwer-Lytton's Rosicrucian novel *Zanoni*, which is based on a famous Victorian esoteric bookshop in Catherine Street, Covent Garden, run by John Denley. Today the number of such shops is sadly dwindling. Some that I have known in other cities include the Table d'Émeraude in the Latin Quarter of Paris and the Librairie Vega nearby in the Boulevard Saint Germain, both sadly long since departed like their San Francisco counterpart, Fields Book Store. R.I.P.

Fig. 2.6. Jeffrey Somers, bookseller extraordinaire, at his shop
Fine Books Oriental in Museum Street, London, 2007.

PHOTOGRAPH BY THE AUTHOR

The London esoteric scene was highly eclectic. Because of the city's sheer size, its role as a metropole, and its cosmopolitan history, it was a crossroads where many different esoteric traditions met and interacted. This was tremendously exciting for someone who wanted to explore the esoteric marketplace. I remember, for example, how in 1977 the first Mind Body Spirit Festival was held at the Olympia exhibition hall in west London. It was a huge event covering every kind of spiritual and esoteric movement and every kind of alternative therapy that one could imagine. And this was the precursor of many similar events. You now find esoteric fairs taking place all over the world, but this must have been one of the very first.

All kinds of other esoteric events were going on all the time. Virtually any night of the week one could go to some event or other—a lecture, a conference, a ritual, a meditation session, a meeting in a pub, or simply a friendly gathering at someone's flat. These events covered an enormous spectrum. They ranged from serious lectures like the ones put on by the Esoteric Society—run by Philip Carr-Gomm, until 2020 leader of the Order of Bards, Ovates and Druids—to a dramatization of part of the *Egyptian Book of the Dead*, put on by the Anthroposophical Chrysalis Theatre Group, to—even more sensational—a public performance of a witchcraft ritual by the self-styled King of the Witches, Alex Sanders, whom I knew briefly. I once attended one of his witchcraft classes at his basement flat in Notting Hill.

Another special thing about this period was the large degree of popular interest in the esoteric, and this was reflected in popular culture. In the pop music scene one saw the Beatles taking up the Maharishi's Transcendental Meditation system and putting Aleister Crowley's face on the cover of their *Sergeant Pepper* album. There was the group Led Zeppelin, led by Crowley admirer Jimmy Page. And there was the musical *Hair*, which opened in London around 1968, with the song "The Age of Aquarius."

Publishers were eager to exploit the boom in public interest in esoteric and occult subjects. One interesting publishing project, which appeared in the early seventies, was called *Man, Myth and Magic*. This was a so-called part-work, or a series of weekly modules that accumulated eventually into a kind of encyclopedia. It was aimed at a mass readership, but the editorial board included some well-known academics, including the archaeologist Glyn Daniel, the anthropologist Mircea Eliade, the psychologist William Sargent, and the scholar of religion R. C. Zaehner. Other similarly distinguished names appeared among the contributors. The result was a curious mixture of the sensational and the serious, but the overall quality was higher than one might have expected. I still possess a set of *Man, Myth and Magic* and refer to it from time to time.

One also saw the beginnings of a scholarly interest in these areas. At that time there was still only a handful of serious scholars working on esoteric subjects, but they were an important handful. One of the key names was Frances Yates at the Warburg Institute, who was coming out with books like *Giordano Bruno and the Hermetic Tradition*, *The Art of Memory*, and *The Rosicrucian Enlightenment*. I remember how exciting it was when these books came out because here was a major scholar, who could not be ignored by the academic community, declaring that the esoteric traditions were important and that the academy could not afford to ignore them any longer. Also at the Warburg was D. P. Walker, author of a seminal work on spiritual and demonic magic. And there were a number of other scholars—both inside and outside academe—writing on esotericism. One was Ellic Howe, whom I got to know well. He had written a book on astrology called *Urania's Children* and went on write *The Magicians of the Golden Dawn*, a classic book on the subject. Ellic was a Freemason, and later on I also became one with his help. Another scholar was Robert A. Gilbert, a Bristol bookseller with an encyclopedic knowledge, who produced important works on the Golden Dawn and the standard biography of A. E. Waite. These were exciting times. I was mixing with fascinating people and had the sense of being part of a pioneering development in the world of scholarship.

3

Meetings with Remarkable People

Meanwhile my own quest continued. By that time I knew quite a lot about the world of esotericism, but was still searching for a personal spiritual path. I had a colleague at *Country Life* who was involved with an offshoot of the Gurdjieff-Ouspensky movement that had taken up the Maharishi Mahesh Yogi's Transcendental Meditation system, then broken with the Maharishi but continued using the system. The colleague arranged for me to be introduced to the group, and I was duly initiated into the meditation technique at the group's headquarters in west London. For a while I dutifully practiced the exercise twice a day and found it effective in inducing a feeling of calm and serenity. However, the group made me feel uneasy. There was something both fanatical and complacent about them. They tried to discourage me from practicing physical yoga, which I had been doing for some time and found beneficial, and my contact there insisted on calling me "McIntosh" as though he were my schoolteacher. Furthermore, my twice daily sessions were interfering with domestic life, so after a few months I gave up the practice.

I went on with my writing career. *The Astrologers and their Creed* was followed by a shorter, more popular book on astrology and then by *Eliphas Lévi and the French Occult Revival*, which came out with Rider in 1972. Next I decided to write a book on the Rosicrucians. In the course of researching for my early books I had become aware of Rosicrucianism as an important current within Western esotericism, and I felt that there was a need for a general history of the movement, as the only comparable work was A. E. Waite's *The Brotherhood of the Rosy Cross*, published in the 1920s and written in Waite's cumbersome prose. I failed to find a publisher willing to commission the work, so I just went ahead and started writing it. The book was later accepted by the Aquarian Press and published as *The Rosy Cross Unveiled*. Subsequently it appeared with the American publisher Weiser as *The Rosicrucians*.

The foreword to the book was written by Colin Wilson, whom I had already met at various esoteric conferences. I came to value him as a friend, and I visited him and his wife, Joy, on a number of occasions at their house at Gorran Haven in Cornwall. I found him a warm and sympathetic person and fascinating to talk to. From a working-class background in Leicester, he had become famous overnight in 1956 with his book *The Outsider*, a study of certain real and fictional characters who were marked by a sense of alienation from the everyday world and an urge to retreat into the world of their own dreams and imagination. For a time he was the darling of the British literary scene. Then the gutter press reported an incident involving a confrontation with Joy's family. It was blown up out of all proportion, but the literary establishment, evidently now embarrassed by their initial enthusiasm, seized on it as an excuse to drop him from favor. It was a classic case of the mob cheering a person one minute and howling for his blood the next. From then on he was never taken seriously by the critics in Britain, although he built up a large following of his own with his novels and books on the occult and other

Fig. 3.1. Colin Wilson at the New York Open Center, circa 1991.
PHOTOGRAPH BY THE AUTHOR

subjects. The episode is an example of the anti-intellectual and anti-metaphysical streak in the British cultural elite, which makes them shy away from anyone who probes too deeply or too challengingly into the realm of ideas or spiritual things.

Around the time that I started working on the Rosicrucian book I also planned to organize a collection of essays by various authors on the subject of techniques of ecstasy and meditation in different religious traditions. In the end the project never went beyond the proposal stage, but it brought me some valued friends. One of them was the already mentioned Jeffrey Somers. At the time I first met him he was about to marry his Japanese fiancée, Nobuko, and the two of them became close friends of mine.

Another close friend I made around this time was Lionel Snell, a Cambridge graduate who had taught mathematics at Eton and was at that time working for the Ministry of Agriculture, Fisheries and Food. He shared my esoteric interests, was an admirer of Aleister Crowley, and knew Gerald Yorke. I immediately found him a kindred spirit and asked him to contribute an essay on magic to the book on techniques of ecstasy. He duly wrote the most original essay on the subject that I had ever read, locating magic in a fourfold scheme along with science, religion, and art, and linked to C. G. Jung's four categories of thinking, feeling, observation, and intuition. When the book project failed to materialize Lionel produced his own self-printed edition of the essay under an imprint that he founded for the purpose called the Mouse that Spins. The book was published anonymously and he gave it the title *S.S.O.T.B.M.E.*, which, for those in the know, stood for "Sex Secrets of the Black Magicians Exposed"—a tongue-in-cheek title typical of Lionel, the point being that this was precisely *not* what the book was about. The book was subsequently taken up by Weiser in the US and appeared in German and Polish editions, becoming a cult classic. Lionel went on to write a whole series of books on magic and related subjects under the pseudonym of Ramsey Dukes, and he is now famous in esoteric circles as a leading magical thinker. Some years ago he emigrated to South Africa along with his South African wife, Lynn McGregor, and now lives near Cape Town.

Yet another key friendship made in the seventies was with the Scottish poet and artist Ian Hamilton Finlay, whom I got to know through writing an article for *Country Life* on Stonypath (later renamed Little Sparta), the remarkable garden that he and his wife Sue had created on a former farm property in the Pentland Hills in Lanarkshire, combining poetry, art, and horticulture. One summer, during a visit to my parents in Edinburgh, I drove out to visit him, not knowing quite what to expect. His poetry had left me rather puzzled, and up to that point gardening had not been a strong interest of mine.

I was full of anticipation as I drove out along the edge of the Pentlands, turned off the main road leading to Lanark, and followed winding side roads up into the hills, past the tiny hamlet of Dunsyre

Fig. 3.2. The Scottish poet and artist
Ian Hamilton Finlay in 1998.

PHOTOGRAPH BY THE AUTHOR

and on until I came to a turning on to a dirt track. There was a farm
gate and a sign to Stonypath with a quotation from Heraclitus: "The
way up and the way down are one and the same." I opened the gate,
drove through, closed the gate behind me, and went on up the dirt
track—a stony path indeed—for about a mile, across a wooden bridge
over a little stream and through another gate, until I came in sight of
some gray stone buildings and a splash of greenery. The effect was of
a small oasis, lost in the bare surrounding hills, but when one entered
the oasis its dimensions seemed miraculously to expand.

Ian came out to the car to meet me—a lean man in his early fifties, with short dark hair, graying slightly, and dark eyes. I sensed immediately that he possessed a powerful charm. He was dressed in a red checked Canadian-style jacket. First he showed me round the gallery, formerly an outbuilding of the farm, containing an exhibition of his works, made by a variety of craftsmen according to his specifications. They incorporated subtle verbal and visual puns, and many of them took the form of military objects like ships and airplanes. One of the items was a game called "Pacific," which he had invented. It was like a complicated version of draughts or checkers, in which the pieces were airplanes, aircraft carriers, and kamikazes. There were even little stools for the players, with planes embroidered on the seats.

After I had seen the gallery he showed me round the garden, and I marveled at what he and Sue had created out of the wilderness of a Lanarkshire hillside. It was full of his creations. In one corner were sculptures of ships—a submarine and two aircraft carriers, one a bird bath and the other a bird table. He said he got great delight from watching the birds landing instead of planes to pick up crumbs in the winter. The garden was full of "wee secret places," as he put it, "a series of little points that go *zing!*"—he said there were not enough of these in the modern world.

That first meeting with Ian had a profound influence on me. For one thing it turned me on to gardens and gardening. What he and Sue had created at Stonypath made me realize that a garden could be a place not only of beauty but also of meaning, a kind of outdoor temple. I was inspired to take up gardening myself, and years later I wrote my book *Gardens of the Gods*, which I dedicated to Ian and which dealt with sacred and symbolic gardens in different cultures. My encounter with Ian and Little Sparta was also important for a different reason, which only became clear to me when I realized that one could experience the ancient gods as more than merely allegorical figures.

Fig. 3.3. The Apollo Temple at Little Sparta.

PHOTOGRAPH BY THE AUTHOR

Ian was a curious mixture: a contemporary artist who rejected modern culture; a radical traditionalist who upheld the virtues of the classical world yet was an admirer of the French Revolution. He was also a kind of Pagan (although he hesitated to describe himself as such) and saw the ancient gods as being more than just mythical motifs with which to decorate a garden. Some years later, in a conversation with me and my then-wife Katherine, he talked about what the gods meant to him. He perceived them as forces in the universe and in ourselves, forces that were denied by what he called the "flower power" mentality. "There are certain things," he said, "that are a given, and forces, different forces, are a part of what's given—that's the gods. And man has to behave as if those forces existed." In this regard Ian certainly practiced what he preached by making Apollo the presiding deity of Little Sparta. An outbuilding serving as a gallery for his works of art was proclaimed to be a temple to Apollo. On the front wall he put trompe l'oeil Corinthian columns and an inscription that said: "TO APOLLO, HIS MUSIC, HIS MISSILES, HIS MUSES." Soon he stopped paying local taxes on the temple, arguing that it was a religious building and therefore tax-exempt. This resulted in a legal battle with the regional authority, which dragged on for years and ended in a sort of stalemate. Over the years he fought many battles—with bureaucracy, the cultural establishment, the media, and so on—some of which I was involved in as a member of his group of supporters, which he called the Saint-Just Vigilantes after the French Revolutionary leader Antoine de Saint-Just. I remained his friend for nearly thirty years until his death in 2006.

By this time I was beginning to discover that I had an aptitude for academic writing that had lain dormant while I was at Oxford. I started to make inquiries about doing a PhD, but my low mark in my Oxford degree proved an obstacle, so I decided to start afresh and do another BA degree. In 1975, at the age of thirty-two, I enrolled in the German department at Birkbeck College, London University, which caters to mature students and has its lectures in the evening. The department occupied a row of houses in Gordon Square, Bloomsbury, one of which had been the home of the economist Maynard Keynes. I plunged eagerly into the study of Goethe, Schiller, Kafka, and Thomas Mann. The faculty members, headed by Professor George Wells, were inspiring, and after just under three years I graduated with a first-class degree.

Meanwhile I made occasional ventures into fiction writing. One of my efforts was what started as a series of short stories, partly inspired by Dion Fortune's story collection, *The Secrets of Dr. Taverner*, featuring a wise doctor who is also a magus. My stories featured a somewhat similar figure called Gilbert North, whom I loosely based on Gerald Yorke, and the narrator was a young journalist called Paul Cairns with a certain resemblance to myself. At a certain point I decided to weave the stories together into a novel. I started writing it for fun and with very little thought of publication, but "books have their fates" as the saying goes, and eventually it was to appear in print, after a long period and a number of revisions, as *Return of the Tetrad*, with the Oxford publisher, Mandrake, run by Chris (Mogg) Morgan.

By the mid-1970s my marriage was coming apart. The ways of the gods are mysterious. They had brought Robin and me together and given us two sons who were and are an infinite joy—and later four wonderful grandchildren. She proved a perfect mother and, for the proverbial seven years, a perfect wife. Then cracks started to appear in the relationship. After the early years of marriage, when a couple is focused inward on each other and the children, there comes a moment when they start to look out at the world again, and sometimes they look out in opposite directions, which is what happened in our case. More and more it became clear that we wanted different things out of life. She was a gregarious person who liked the whirl of social life, parties, and dancing to loud pop music—all of which I could only take in small doses. Furthermore, she could not share the spiritual quest that I was pursuing. Increasingly our lives, interests, and friendships diverged.

Eventually, in 1978, things came to a head and I moved out of Berkhamsted and into a flat that I had bought in Tufnell Park, north London. Coincidentally, at the same time I left *Country Life* and started a new job as assistant editor at the *Illustrated London News*, a prestigious monthly magazine. There I became almost immediately the object of a vicious conspiracy against me by certain members of the staff, and the editor failed to give me the support that he should have done. The result was that I left after about six months. A decade or so later the magazine went into a decline and ceased publication in 2003, by which time I had built a new and much more satisfying career elsewhere. The editor in question has long since died, and at this point in time I prefer to let sleeping dogs lie. On the plus side I managed to write a couple of articles for the magazine, which stood me in good stead for the future. There followed some five years as a freelance editor and writer, mostly for the London publisher Mitchell Beazley.

One of my first freelance assignments was to write an article on Munich for the *Illustrated London News,* the editor having agreed to the article while I was still working there. I was able to combine the trip with some research for a biography of King Ludwig II of Bavaria, which had been commissioned by the publishing firm of Allen Lane. I came to the subject of Ludwig through my love for the music of Richard Wagner, whom Ludwig had idolized and generously supported at critical times in Wagner's life. I read Wilfrid Blunt's shortish, beautifully illustrated book on Ludwig, *The Dream King,* and was struck by Blunt's comment that a more detailed biography was called for. I felt the time had come for me to branch out from the esoteric area, and King Ludwig seemed like a good subject. While in Munich I visited Ludwig's famous castles— Neuschwanstein, Linderhof, and Herrenchiemsee, as well as the spot on Lake Starnberg where he and his doctor had drowned under mysterious circumstances.

I also attended a memorable performance of *Lohengrin* at the Munich Opera House with the American tenor James King in the title role. I had already heard *Lohengrin* on record, but now on stage I experienced the full glory of the opera. From the first notes of the prelude I felt myself swept along by wave upon wave of spellbinding sound—now soft and wistful, now surging to a great orgasmic crescendo. Decades later I learned that my maternal grandmother, as a young woman on a tour of Europe, had been to a performance of *Lohengrin* in Berlin at the time of Kaiser Wilhelm and had described it as the most beautiful thing she had heard on the trip. In King Ludwig's case too it was *Lohengrin* that made him into a Wagner devotee. So how could I not be entranced by it? Ever since then it has been my favorite opera.

Soon after returning to London I gave a lecture on Ludwig at Birkbeck College, and there I met a German woman called Gisela, a student in the German department who had enrolled a couple of years after me, and worked as a freelance translator. She had a wistful, dreamy aura and, like myself, a romantic view of the world, so not surprisingly we found each other kindred spirits and started a love affair.

Almost from the start it was full of conflict, but there were happy interludes. In the spring of 1981 I spent a couple of months in Paris to write a guidebook that had been commissioned by Mitchell Beazley, and Gisela joined me there for part of the time, as did my sons Angus and Jason, who had grown into two very lively teenagers. We lived in a tiny, charming rented flat in Montmartre belonging to Robert Jaulin, an anthropologist, and his wife. One of the contacts we had there was Robert Amadou, a Freemason and writer on esotericism who was also a priest of the Syrian Church. With his beard, long black robe, and sandals, he cut a picturesque figure in the streets of Paris. His much younger wife, Katharina, dressed rather like a nun. Later he wrote a foreword to the French edition of my book on the Rosicrucians.

Despite these pleasant intervals the relationship with Gisela was always precarious. Several times I broke it off and then relented. At that time I had little knowledge of psychology; otherwise I would have recognized that she was seriously mentally disturbed, although she concealed it very skillfully. It was one of those destructive relationships in which the parties can live neither with each other nor without each other. After about two stormy years I thought to resolve things by our getting married, and she moved into my flat in September 1981. It was the worst decision I ever made, as I soon realized. There were constant rows, some of them bitter and ugly, and as a consequence I was developing an ugly side to my character.

In the summer of 1982 I had a brief respite when I attended a weekend workshop on Rosicrucianism led by Gareth Knight, held at Hawkwood College in Gloucestershire, an Anthroposophical center housed in a stately mansion, set in lovely grounds. I drove down there on a beautiful summer day with two friends. One was Adam McLean, publisher of the periodical *Hermetic Journal* and an esoteric book series called Magnum Opus Hermetic Sourceworks. The other was Marion Green, already mentioned as editor of the journal *Quest* and organizer of esoteric conferences. On the way to Hawkwood College we stopped off at Forthampton Court, which was open to the public for the day, and had tea with Gerald Yorke. After we arrived we sat for a while on the terrace overlooking the garden, which was suffering from the very dry weather. As we were sitting there one of the visitors, a middle-aged woman, remarked how sad it was that some of the flowers were dying. Yorke's reply was: "Yes, but it's rather nice when sad things happen." We went on to the workshop at Hawkwood College, which was a marvelous event, charismatically led by Gareth Knight and with a very interesting group of participants including Dolores Ashcroft-Novicki, John and Caitlin Matthews, and Robert Stewart. Then after the workshop it was back to the flat in London, to more bitter rows, sleepless nights, and frayed nerves.

At the same time the gods were bringing certain key influences to bear on my life, which would prove crucial for my subsequent journey. One day, when I was still living alone in the flat, a young American called Marion Redd paid me a visit, having been put in touch with me by a friend of his in the United States with whom I had been corresponding. Marion was a Freemason and deeply interested in matters Hermetic and Rosicrucian, and I immediately found him a kindred spirit. It was around this time that I myself became a Freemason through contacts provided by Ellic Howe. I entered the Pilgrim Lodge, an old-established lodge that has the unusual feature of conducting its ceremonies in German, having been founded by German courtiers and merchants in 1779. I found the ceremonies very beautiful and I enjoyed the friendships that Freemasonry brought me.

New friendships also came in other ways. For a time Gisela and I were running a mail-order esoteric book business called Orpheus Books, and one morning in early 1982 a young, fair-haired Icelander called Hilmar Örn Hilmarsson came to the door and asked to see our stock. He was my first real contact with the land of the Vikings. He spoke rather softly, with a quicksilver quality of charm and humor, combined with an agility in the English language that would have been the envy of many a native English speaker. He appeared to have read every esoteric book ever published, including my *Eliphas Lévi and the French Occult Revival*. It was clear to me right away that he was a kindred spirit. In no time we were deep in conversation, and he stayed on for lunch. That was the start of a friendship that has lasted to this day. Hilmar is now famous as a composer of film music and as the leader of the Asatru community in Iceland—that is, those who follow the old Nordic gods. I was later to follow him into Asatru. There were times when we lost touch, but he always reappeared in my life through remarkable happenstance, as I shall relate.

Another important experience was connected with a sort of commune called the Enclave that occupied a house in St. George's Avenue, Tufnell Park, close to where we lived. Most of the members were esoterically minded, and they had fitted out the basement as a temple for use by a magical group of which Gisela and I were both members. We practiced a form of ceremonial magic, loosely based on that of the Hermetic Order of the Golden Dawn. The group, led by a Cambridge classics graduate called Charlie Ebbutt, was a mixed bag in terms of age and social background. One of the members was the American anthropologist Tanya Luhrmann, who had joined in order to do research on modern witchcraft and ritual magic in England for her Cambridge doctoral thesis, later to be published as *Persuasions of the Witch's Craft.*

Another member was Ellie Niemeyer, a young Dutch woman who was also the leader of the commune. She had a forceful, arresting personality and a steely will, honed by nine years in the harsh conditions of a series of children's homes in Holland, where she was protected, as she believed, by occult forces. Subsequently she had embarked on a spiritual journey that had taken her through spiritualism, the Rosicrucian Order AMORC, and witchcraft. After moving to England, she had learned the language from scratch and spoke a colorful version of it, tinged with bits of London slang. Anyone who had more than a passing acquaintance with her could tell that she had a warm and generous heart. One day she announced excitedly to the group that she had discovered the runes and with them her true path. She went on to embrace the Nordic gods passionately and adopted the name Freya Aswynn. Under that name she wrote an excellent book on the runes called *Leaves of Yggdrasil* and is now known as one of the leading experts worldwide on the Nordic religion. On one occasion, when I was in the middle of a crisis in my life and was tempted to take a desperate step, she carried out a rune reading for me and got the message: "Don't do a damn thing!" I followed her advice and probably thereby avoided an even worse situation. She played a part in steering me in the direction of the runes and the Nordic tradition, but that was to come later.

Not far away from the Enclave was another house where the mysteries were celebrated under the leadership of Zachary Cox and Jean Morton-Williams, a remarkable couple who also became good friends of mine. They were leading members of an organization called the Pagan Federation, which has played a major role in getting Pagans recognized as a legitimate religious community in Britain. They lived in a big, red brick Victorian or Edwardian house on a steep road run-

Fig. 3.4. Zachary Cox and Jean Morton-Williams.
For many decades their house in north London was a
vibrant center for the mysteries.

PHOTOGRAPH BY RUTH BAYER

ning down from Highgate to Crouch End, where they let out a couple of rooms to like-minded tenants. As soon as you entered you sensed that something unusual and exciting was afoot there. Several different magical and pagan groups met at the house, and the living room at the back was constantly in use as a temple. There every so often they performed Crowley's Gnostic Mass, which I attended a few times. In the basement was a printing press where Zach produced a magazine called *Aquarian Arrow*. The focal point for socializing was the dining room, which doubled as a sort of common room. It was the scene of convivial meals and ad hoc gatherings, where Pagans and esotericists of all persuasions talked animatedly for hours on end, fortified by endless cups of strong tea. Tanya Luhrmann also frequented the house and describes it in *Persuasions of the Witch's Craft*.

During those years ritual magic was an important part of my life, so what attracted me to it? First of all, it fulfilled the soul's need for journeys into enchantment. The process of "disenchanting the world," of which Max Weber spoke, is one of the most damaging things that have come with the secularization of society, and magic is one attempt to restore that enchantment. So what is ritual magic and how does it work? Essentially, it is the use of certain symbols, images, sensory experiences, and ritual formulae, charged by the imagination and put to the service of the will to bring about changes in oneself or in the world. This is something we experience in our ordinary lives in different ways. A formal dinner party with its candlelight, soft music, festive table, and ceremonially served food is a kind of ritual magic, designed to induce a certain mood in the participants. So is an orchestral concert—think of the hushed moment when the conductor, in his white tie and tails, raises his baton, a kind of magic wand, and signals to the musicians to begin playing. A theatrical performance, a football match, a political rally, and a press conference are all forms of magical ritual, although most people would not think of them that way. Ritual magic proper is a heightened form of the same thing, namely the acting out of a system of symbolism in a ceremonial context.

But there is an even more profound aspect to ritual. At the risk of oversimplification let's consider the human being as having a body, a conscious mind, and an unconscious mind. The connection between the unconscious mind and the body is far stronger than between the unconscious and the conscious mind. This is why, when you experience a sudden fright or emotional shock, your body reacts before your conscious mind does. I remember my American maternal grandmother relating how, on a visit to London, she was walking near the Houses of Parliament and suddenly found herself standing in front of a statue of Abraham Lincoln. In that instant her hand flew up involuntarily to make the sign of the cross. Seeing the statue of the great American hero, she instinctively reacted by making a religious gesture. The same thing can work in reverse. If you want to reach the deeper levels of the mind, an effective way to do so is through symbolically charged gestures, movements, and sounds. This is the essence of ritual magic.

Basically what we try to do in magic is to use our imaginations and wills creatively in order to achieve an ideal. Let us suppose that our ideal is to bring about a balance within ourselves. The first thing we have to do is to understand what it is that needs to be balanced, what forces in us are conflicting. Each of these forces is given a name and certain characteristics and images that are associated with it. We then build up a system of images that we can manipulate with our imaginations. And we become more skilled at this the more famil-iar we become with the system we are using. To signify the different stages of development in a person's mastery of the system we have a series of grades of initiation. Finally we have a set of rituals, some of which we use for initiation to the grades, some for invoking particu-lar symbols within the system.

This essentially describes my own approach to magic at the time when I was involved with the group in London. The material we worked with was basically in the tradition of the Hermetic Order of the Golden Dawn and included the elements, the compass directions, the planets, and the spheres of the Kabbalistic Tree of Life. While I found it extremely beautiful and uplifting, ultimately I found it too abstract, too unconnected with the world of nature, and too remote from my own roots and cultural background. However, it was an important step on my path and one that taught me a great deal.

4

Restless Years

In the meantime the relationship with Gisela continued to be full of stress. The year after she moved in I was able to get away for a few months to Washington, DC, to write a book on the city for a new series of travel guides, published jointly by Mitchell Beazley and American Express. I broke my journey in Iceland to visit Hilmar, write an article on the country, and give two lectures that Hilmar had arranged—one on the Rosicrucians and the other on King Ludwig—and was totally enchanted by Iceland. It is a place where you feel particularly strongly the power of the four classical elements. Watching a geyser, we saw how fire, deep in the earth, sent hot water bursting out and mingling with the air in great clouds of steam in a wonderful combination of the elements.

Water subjected us to a special ordeal. We set out to visit the remains of a Viking farmhouse at Stöng that had been preserved under volcanic ash for several centuries and had recently been excavated. We were driving along in Hilmar's car through a wild inland region to the east of Reykjavik when we came to a fast-flowing river where a ford was the only way to cross over. Hilmar bravely drove the car into the water, and halfway across it stuck and the motor stalled.

He tried the ignition and the car gave a splutter and remained still. After a few more attempts the engine fired and we drove to the other side. We went on to visit the farmhouse, then had to return across the river by the same ford, and again the car stalled in the middle. This time all Hilmar's attempts to start the engine failed. Ice-cold water was flowing into the car and over my feet. Worse still, it appeared that the exhaust pipe was also underwater and this was preventing the engine from starting. We changed places. Hilmar said I should try to start the engine while he lifted up the back end of the car. He waded into the water and round to the back. By now the pedals were also underwater. I looked over my shoulder and saw Hilmar straining to lift the car, and in that moment I activated the ignition and pressed the accelerator. Miracle! The engine started and I was able to drive the car up on to the bank, with the floor under several inches of water. Evidently the car had been built for such an eventuality, because there was a drainage hole in the floor with a sort of bath plug in it. Hilmar pulled out the plug, the water flowed out, and we went on our way. Subsequently two of the tires burst from the damage they had sustained in the river and had to be replaced.

A day or two later I boarded a plane for New York, where I met my elder son, Angus, who was there on holiday. We met at the flat of my maternal uncle, John Bainbridge, and then traveled down to Baltimore to stay with his son, John Junior. After Angus flew home I went to Washington and stayed in lodgings with a pleasant woman called Mila. The house, similar to an old New York brownstone, was on Rhode Island Avenue, close to Logan Circle, an area much frequented by hookers, who paraded up and down the surrounding streets and would sometimes stop me and ask if I wanted a "date." I borrowed a bicycle from Mila's son and pedaled around the city from one tourist attraction to the next, and by December I had covered all the major sites. I interrupted the stay in Washington and flew out to Los Angeles where I stayed with a rich widow who ran a club to raise money for cultural restoration projects in France. By then my book on King Ludwig had come out, and I gave a lecture on him at her club, but relations with her went sour. I moved out and stayed with an eccentric English poet friend who lived in a Spanish-style bungalow in a sprawling district of similar houses, drinking English tea, writing nostalgic poems about England, and feeling alienated from LA. After a side trip to San Francisco I went back to Washington to finish the book. When I got back to London I discovered that Mitchell Beazley had shelved the publication, albeit with some prospect that it would be revived in the future.

Domestically things got better for a while. When I arrived home from Washington Gisela and I had a reconciliation, and for a few months we lived sufficiently harmoniously that we were able to go on holiday together to Greece in the spring of 1983. We flew to Athens, where we spent a couple of days, then traveled by bus around the Peloponnese. One of the highlights was going to the ancient healing center of Epidaurus, dedicated to Asklepios, god of medicine. In ancient times, if you went there to be cured you would end your stay by spending a night in an underground chamber, where you would go to sleep confidently expecting that Asklepios would appear to you in a dream and tell you the remedy for your complaint.

Another highlight was visiting a monastery in the mountains of the central Peloponnese. From the main road we walked steeply down the side of a deep river valley via many hairpin bends. Vast cliffs plunged abruptly down to the river. On our side, far down to the right, we could just see some of the monastery buildings. From here a footpath led down through some trees and up again along a cliff edge. Then suddenly we found ourselves by the monastery, which was built against an overhanging cliff with some of the rooms perched on precarious-looking wooden balconies. A horse was grazing quietly in an enclosure, a bell round its neck tinkling gently. In the courtyard of the monastery was a big sycamore tree. Sunlight filtered through the leaves of the surrounding sycamores and other trees. We sat down on a bench by the gate and soon an elderly man came and invited us into the monastery where we were taken into a little old-fashioned parlor and given coffee and biscuits by a young, dark-haired, bearded monk. He told us he had been there ten years and that there were fifteen monks there. He spoke no English, but I had taken the trouble to learn some tourist Greek before the journey, so we were able to have a conversation of sorts.

More and more I have come to value such places, set apart from the everyday world, where the soul can find peace, beauty, and inner refreshment. Later I had a similar feeling when visiting Buddhist monasteries in the mountains of Korea. There is something about the presence of mountains that I find conducive to this kind of atmosphere. One of my favorite films, *Lost Horizon*, is about such a place—an idyllic sanctuary hidden away in the Himalayas.

You might expect that a trip filled with such magic moments would strengthen our relationship, but once we were back in London all the old conflicts started up again. By that summer I was at the end of my tether and knew that I had to take drastic action. Morally I felt I couldn't throw Gisela out of the flat, as she had invested a lot of money in its renovation, but I was afraid that if I stayed I would reach my breaking point. So one day I walked out and went to live in lodgings in Hampstead. Fortunately I had kept delaying the planned marriage, and it never took place.

It was at that point that I started writing a novel called *The Devil's Claw*, set in the early part of the twentieth century and involving a group of nine people who had been together in previous incarnations. Eight members of the group come together in London and are convinced that the missing ninth member has gone down an evil path and needs to be stopped. Gradually it becomes clear that the ninth member has become incarnated as Adolf Hitler. I worked on the story for about six years and submitted it to most of the major London publishers through my agent, but none of them took it—understandably, because I now realize that it has a number of major flaws.

Over two years I moved about nine times, staying with friends or in rented lodgings. It was a precarious existence, but paradoxically it was a richly exciting time. That summer I went to Wolfenbüttel in Germany to visit a Masonic brother and do some research in the Herzog August Library, where Leibniz had been librarian. From there I went down to Lower Austria to stay with a couple who lived in a semi-disused Dominican monastery in Retz. Then I went to Vienna to get a night train back in the direction of home. Having a few hours to spare before the train left, I visited some friends near Schönbrunn Palace. We drank tea by candlelight, and it must have put me into a heightened state of mind—like with the madeleine dipped in tea that Marcel Proust writes about in *À la recherche du temps perdu*—because in the tram to the West Station I was floating on a cloud of bliss.

In such a state magical things tend to happen. On the train I found myself in a sleeping compartment with two women, one of them a pretty and vivacious girl in her twenties called Regina, with whom I got into conversation. Next morning we heard that there was a rail strike in Belgium and that the train would not proceed beyond Aachen. What was I to do? It was then I remembered that Ingrid, my old au pair and fairy godmother, lived somewhere near Bonn. After giving Regina my address in London I left the train at Bonn and called Ingrid from a telephone box. Could she put me up? Of course she could, and an hour or so later she arrived at the station and drove me to her house up in the hills above Bad Honnef. Outwardly a rather plain, one-story house, inside it was filled with beautiful antiques and works of art and had an atmosphere of—to use a German expression—*heile Welt* (a world that is whole). We had not seen each other for over twenty years, so it was a moving reunion for both of us.

Back in London I stayed for several months in a flat in Addison Road, Holland Park, belonging to my old friend Jeffrey Somers and his Japanese wife, Nobuko. They were among the friends who were a tremendous support to me during this difficult time. Not far away in Kensington was Eva Loewe, an Austrian woman married to a Spaniard. I got to know Eva when we both took part in a course at the Westminster Pastoral Foundation given by the psychologist and writer Noel Cobb—I forget the exact subject, but I believe it was something to do with the divine feminine.

We soon developed a strong rapport, although it never developed into a love affair. She was a follower of the German guru Thorwald Dethlefsen and asked me to help her translate Dethlefsen's book *Schicksal als Chance*, which appeared in our translation as *The Challenge of Fate*. Dethlefsen believed that each person is responsible for everything that happens to them—even apparent accidents. During the course of translating his book I became strongly influenced by his philosophy, as I wrote in my diary at the time: "D's philosophy is extremely difficult to accept in its totality, but if one tries suspending disbelief it becomes wonderfully bracing and liberating. . . . When I split up with Gisela the problem of the flat seemed insoluble because I saw myself as the victim of a disaster. When I asked myself what this was trying to teach me I realized that fate was working against my tendency to get stuck in a groove, jogging me, pushing me on." Nowadays I am skeptical about Dethlefsen, but perhaps even the strangest ideas can act as a valuable catalyst if they appear at the appropriate moment in one's life. Dethlefsen's notion of Stoic acceptance of the messages of fate led me to let go of the Tufnell Park flat and eventually reach an agreement that Gisela would buy it from me.

It was around this time that I became involved in the founding of a society comprising a group of friends interested in esoteric matters. The main initiator was Gerald Suster, Cambridge graduate, occultist, and writer. Of partly Russian Jewish extraction, Gerald was a self-assertive, talkative, amusing person with a belligerent side that frequently caused him to pick quarrels, make enemies, and fall out with friends—although not with me.

One evening Gerald brought together a group of his friends at the Museum Tavern in Great Russell Street opposite the British Museum to propose the creation of a learned society with a broadly esoteric focus. One of those present was Nicholas Goodrick-Clarke, who had taken an Oxford doctorate with a thesis that was later published under the title *The Occult Roots of Nazism*. Nicholas made a strong impression on me from the start with his powerful charm and charisma, his humor, his loud, infectious laugh, and his flow of sparkling, brilliant talk.

We went ahead and founded "the Society"—we could never agree on any other name, so "the Society" it remained. The early meetings were held just around the corner from the Museum Tavern at another pub called the Plough where we met in an upstairs room, sustained by drinks from the bar downstairs. At one of the first meetings I gave a talk on one of my favorite writers, Gustav Meyrink, author of *The Golem*.

Some of the talks at subsequent meetings included Nicholas Goodrick-Clarke on the occult roots of Nazism, Ellic Howe on the Ordo Templi Orientis, Eric Towers on Sir Francis Dashwood and the Hellfire Club, Timothy d'Arch Smith on Montague Summers, Gerald Suster on the Golden Dawn, and Paul Baines on alchemy. Paul, whom I had gotten to know through our mutual friend the alchemical and Hermetic scholar Adam McLean, earned his basic living as an embalmer, but he also practiced as a herbalist, and his real passion was making alchemical remedies according to the Paracelsian method known as spagyric alchemy, involving processing a plant to produce a calx, an oil, and a tincture, and then reuniting these to create a powerful medicine. At one time I did a bit of alchemy myself and learned a lot from watching Paul at work. Sadly, he died relatively young, having suffered for many years from a bone disease.

Another Society member was Michael Cox, at that time a commissioning editor with the esoteric publisher the Aquarian Press,

Fig. 4.1. Members of "the Society" on a Golden Dawn tour of
London, c. 1987. (*Left to right*) *Back row*: Unidentified woman,
Martin Etough, Geraldine Collins, Michael Cox.
Front row: Nicholas Goodrick-Clarke, Christopher Wolstenholme,
Robert Gilbert, Gerald Suster, Kathleen Collins, Jessica Johnson,
John Hamill, Paul Baynes, unidentified man.

PHOTOGRAPH BY THE AUTHOR

who was then working on a biography of the ghost story writer
M. R. James. One of our meetings was held shortly before Christmas
and, to make a change from the usual lecture, Michael read aloud
one of James's ghost stories. To heighten the atmosphere we had the
room at the Plough lit by candlelight. The only trouble was that the
landlord of the pub evidently thought we were holding a black mass,
because after that we were banned from the Plough and moved our
meetings first to a pub in Rathbone Place off Oxford Street and then
to one in Maida Vale.

The Society also organized excursions, one of which was a
tour of London sites associated with the Hermetic Order of the

Golden Dawn. Another was to Stourhead in Wiltshire, with its remarkable park, based on the account of Aeneas's journey around the Mediterranean, as described in Virgil's *Aeneid*. By that time, inspired by Ian Hamilton Finlay's garden, I had developed an interest in sacred and symbolic gardens and had started to collect material for what later became my book *Gardens of the Gods*.

5

Second Marriage and Oxford Revisited

The two vagabond years were full of excitement and rich experience. In early 1984 I got a postcard from Regina, the woman I had met on the train from Vienna, to say that she was coming to England. I invited her to stay in the Holland Park flat, and we started a wonderful love affair. She was full of energy and sparkle and a delight to be with. The affair lasted about eight or nine months. I stayed with her in Cologne, where she lived, we had a holiday in Portugal together, and she came back to London a couple of times to visit me. She wanted us to settle down together and start a family, but in the end it was clear to me that it wouldn't work. She was a committed Catholic with religious views very different from mine, which I think were puzzling to her, and in the long run this would have led to a serious rift.

During this time I was twice employed as a lecturer on a Swedish cruise ship, the *Lindblad Polaris*, taking tourists around various historic cities of Europe. My task was to lecture on the history of these places. The first trip, in the spring of 1984, went from Lisbon to

Copenhagen, and I took the opportunity to visit my brother, David, who was running a factory in Oporto for the textile firm Coats. Regina joined me there and we went on to Lisbon together, then she went home and I joined the cruise ship. In the autumn of the same year I went on another cruise, this time from Copenhagen to Lisbon. On that second trip, when we docked at London close to Tower Bridge, I held a lunch party on board. My American cousin William Sims Bainbridge happened to be visiting London at that time with his then-partner Katherine Kurs, so I invited them to the lunch, along with Angus, Jason, my sister June, and her husband Terry. Bill was a sociology professor at Harvard and a well-known expert on religious cults. After a convivial lunch, cousin Bill, Katherine, and I walked down to Tower Bridge and went up to the gallery joining the two towers. I sensed a rapport with Katherine straight away. She combined attractive looks with a quiet warmth and a kind of deep, thoughtful quality. I said goodbye to them before returning to the ship, not thinking I would see Katherine again. I was wrong.

Meanwhile I continued to move from one temporary accommodation to the next. From Holland Park I moved to a rented room in West Hampstead, then shared a flat in Notting Hill with Hilmar Hilmarsson, who was living temporarily in London. From there I moved into the house of Zachary and Jean in Crouch End, and spent several enjoyable months in their hive of occult activity with its constant round of meetings and rituals, some of which I took part in. Soon after moving in there I was pleasantly surprised to receive a letter from Katherine, and we entered into a correspondence.

In the summer of 1985 my two years of wandering around London came to an end when I bought a flat in Avenell Road, Highbury, close to the Arsenal football stadium, having sold the Tufnell Park flat to Gisela. By then I had found a job as an editor with Mitchell Beazley, for whom I had been working already for some years as a freelancer. Soon after I took the job, the Washington project was resurrected, and I was sent back there to update it.

I arrived in Washington around January 1986 and stayed for the first few days in Georgetown with my friend Andrew Gray, translator of Wagner's autobiography *Mein Leben*, whom I had gotten to know on my previous visit to Washington. Through an accommodation agency I quickly found lodgings with Lisa Ritchie, a poet and short story writer who was active in the Washington literary scene and held two writers' workshops every week. She lived with her partner and later husband, Clyde Farnsworth, a prominent writer on economic matters for the *New York Times* and a keen violinist. They occupied a beautiful, spacious, red-brick, nineteenth-century house in Cleveland Park, a lovely, leafy district near Washington Cathedral. I had a big attic room with a desk and a telephone—ideal conditions for working on the guidebook. Lisa and Clyde became good friends and have remained so over the years. I attended some of her writers' meetings, and they involved me in their social life. On one occasion they took me to an "opera party" where you had to appear as a character from an opera and sing a line from the work before a panel of experts, who then had to identify the character. If they failed then you won a prize. For me the choice was obvious—I decided to go as Lohengrin. From a theatrical shop I bought a plastic Roman helmet and managed to convert it into a reasonable Lohengrin helmet by taking off the plume and turning up the earflaps so they looked like wings. Lisa lent me a sort of Indian waistcoat, which made a good tunic when worn back to front, and a coat with a red lining, which I turned inside out to make a cloak. Accompanied by Clyde on the violin, I sang the opening of Lohengrin's soliloquy "In fernem Land," which the panel identified straightaway.

An interesting acquaintance I made at this time was Gary Davis, who lived in the basement of Lisa's house and was quite famous as an advocate of world government. He wanted to do away with

Fig. 5.1. Myself as the Grail knight Lohengrin at a fancy dress opera party in Washington, DC.
PHOTOGRAPH FROM THE AUTHOR'S COLLECTION

nation-states and have only two levels of government: global and local. He had an office in Washington with a staff of about four people. By joining his organization one became a "world citizen" and received a world passport, which was recognized by many countries. I found Gary very likeable and entertaining, and briefly I toyed with the idea of becoming a world citizen, but what gave me pause was the fear of what would happen if the world government became a tyranny—then there would be no escape from it. In the light of world developments since then, my fear was well founded. We are rapidly moving toward a world tyranny—the tyranny of international business and finance, which is a law unto itself, unconstrained by national interests and indifferent to everything except the bottom line on the balance sheet. I shall return to this topic later, as the phenomenon of globalization became a major bête noire of mine.

The Washington sojourn marked a key turning point in my life. After a few weeks there I began to dread going back to the numbing toil of my publishing job in London, and I conceived the idea of moving to the States and taking up an academic career. The idea was a small seed from which great changes were about to grow. One weekend I went up to Cambridge, Massachusetts, to visit my cousin Bill Bainbridge, who was teaching sociology at Harvard University. Bill was and is a kindred spirit. He specialized in the sociology of fringe religious sects and among other things had written a book, sensationally entitled *Satan's Power*, about the Process movement, which had started as an offshoot of Scientology and involved the worship of four deities—Christ, Jehovah, Lucifer, and Satan—who could be combined in different pairs to designate different human types. Thus one could be a Christ-Jehovah type, a Jehovah-Lucifer type, a Lucifer-Satan type, and so on. Bill had joined the Process in order to do the research for the book and had retained an affection for the group, as indicated by various Process relics around his flat, such as a curiously shaped wooden altar. We discussed my germ of an idea about coming to the US and entering academe, and he was very encouraging.

We had Sunday brunch at a restaurant called Pistachio's with his Japanese girlfriend (later wife), Erika, and Katherine, with whom I had been corresponding since our meeting on board the cruise ship. I gathered that she was in a relationship with an Episcopal priest, but that they were just in the process of splitting up. Next day we had dinner together and things sparked between us, although we didn't actually start a love affair until she came down to Washington a week or two later. Washington in the springtime is a wonderful place, especially when you're in love. Katherine was about to complete a graduate degree in religion and theology at Harvard Divinity School, and very soon we were talking about a future together, although it wasn't clear how we were going to manage it with the Atlantic between us.

The following month, April 1986, I returned to the US for a lecture tour that had been organized for me by a lecture agent called Wallace Dow, who lived near Baltimore. The first talk, at a country club, was a disaster, as I was part of a double bill. The first part was taken up by a pianist and cabaret artist who gave such a stunning performance that my lecture afterward came as an anticlimax. It went much better at the next three venues: a retirement home near Baltimore, Bridgewater College in Virginia, and the Tuckahoe Woman's Club in Richmond, Virginia. From Richmond, Wallace Dow drove me up to Washington, where I took a plane from Dulles Airport to Boston, where Katherine and Bill met me at the airport and took me to Bill's flat in Cambridge, where he kindly allowed Katherine and me to stay. We had a wonderful week together, marred only by the news of the Chernobyl nuclear disaster in Ukraine.

I flew back to London and a few weeks later Katherine, having received her degree, joined me and we decided to get married. It was a marvelous and eventful summer. We spent a few days with my parents in Edinburgh and took the opportunity to visit Ian Hamilton Finlay, with whom Katherine got on very well—a highly fruitful meeting for her, as it later turned out. I applied to Oxford to do my doctorate there and was accepted by the history faculty and given a place at my old college, Christ Church. My supervisor was to be Robert Evans of Brasenose College, who was an expert on central European history and had written, among other things, a book on the emperor Rudolf II, dealing in depth with Rudolf's esoteric interests. He was therefore an ideal supervisor for the subject I had chosen: the eighteenth-century Golden and Rosy Cross Order.

Katherine and I set our marriage date for near the end of October, and meanwhile Katherine flew back to the States for a major back operation. She had suffered for most of her life from scoliosis, curvature of the spine, which had been getting steadily worse and caused her to lose height. The operation, conducted in Boston, involved a complete fusion of all the spine vertebrae, which the surgeon told her was the only way to prevent the curvature from becoming worse. After the operation she was suffering from a lot of pain, and I flew over to the States to give her moral support, staying with my cousin Bill, who by now was living with Erika. When Katherine was well enough she flew back to England, and we went straight from the airport to the registry office at Finsbury Town Hall where we went through a civil marriage. From there we drove to Oxford and moved into a flat owned by Christ Church, located in Abbey Road near the station.

Not content with just a civil marriage, we wanted to marry in a religious context but design our own ceremony, so we decided the best option was a Unitarian church, as the Unitarians are known for being highly nondogmatic. The minister of the Unitarian Chapel in Rosslyn Hill, Hampstead, a genial Australian called David Usher, agreed to moderate the ceremony, while giving us a completely free hand to conduct it in our own way. We wanted to dress up a bit for the occasion, so we had tabards made out of a shiny, silk-like material, Katherine's in silver, mine in dark blue. On the breast of each was an emblem in the form of an overlapping sun and moon, in gold and pale blue, with the rays forming a cross and the letter *K*, the moon suggesting a *C*. When I took the material to a Greek tailor in Soho, he looked at the design in astonishment and said: "I don't believe it! You're getting married and you're wearing this! What is it? Is it religion?" Nevertheless, he made the tabards for us, and we put them on at the point in the ceremony when we were about to take our marriage vows. The ceremony itself, attended by close friends and my two sons, was an eclectic mixture, including readings from Swinburne's poem "Hertha" (*I am that which began, out of me the years roll / Out of me God and Man, I am equal and whole*), John Donne's "The

Good Morrow," part of Aleister Crowley's Gnostic Mass, the Lord's Prayer, and the prayer to Our Mother from one of the Gnostic gospels. We also had a kind of communion in which the congregation stood in a circle and each person was given a glass of wine. Afterward we had a celebration dinner at a restaurant across the road. The same evening we drove back to Oxford, and the following day we drove off for a short honeymoon in the Malvern area, paying a visit to the Rollright Stones on the way home.

Back in Oxford, at the age of forty-three, I embarked on my DPhil thesis. As I proceeded I discussed each chapter with Robert Evans, and I also took the opportunity to pick the brains of some other distinguished Oxford scholars. One of them was Sir Isiah Berlin, the eminent philosopher, intellectual historian, and expert on the Enlightenment and Counter-Enlightenment, which was the area of my thesis. After giving me a very clear account of the basic characteristics of the Enlightenment, he went on to remark that the whole Enlightenment project had now essentially come to an end. I think he must have been very dismayed by the direction that politics were taking in the era of Thatcher and Reagan, which was then in full swing.

Things were rather tight for us financially. I had sold the flat in Highbury, but the proceeds were not quite enough to see me through the doctorate, so I continued to work for Mitchell Beazley on a reduced basis, commuting into London three days a week. At first it was heaven being back in Oxford—working in the Bodleian Library, dining in the magnificent Great Hall of Christ Church, strolling through college quadrangles and along the Cherwell River, going to Brasenose for tutorials with Robert Evans. Then, after a while, certain things about Oxford began to irk me. I was of course much older than any of the other students, even the graduates, so there was no social life to be had there. On the other hand, I didn't really fit into the world of the dons. There were times when I felt isolated and irritated by the cliquish and arrogant side of Oxford. And it was not as though the town of Oxford offered much. Apart from the university and the colleges, Oxford is a rather humdrum town. However, toward the end of our stay I began to warm to the place again. It could offer some enchanting moments, especially in autumn and winter at twilight when soft lights would go on in wood-paneled, book-lined college rooms, and you would get glimpses of little groups of people gathering for predinner drinks.

Friendships were few, but one of them was with Karina Williamson, an English don at St. Hilda's College, whose late husband had been a colleague of my father's—later she was to become my father's second wife. Another friendship was with Charles Webster, a distinguished historian of science from All Souls College, and his wife, Carol. We also befriended the American historian David Sorkin of St. Anthony's College and his wife, Shifra.

Other friends would come from elsewhere to visit us. One was Freya Aswynn. She came for the day and we took her punting on the river Cherwell. At that time she was working on her book *Leaves of Yggdrasil*, and I remember that the title occurred to her as we were walking through the streets of Oxford. Soon afterward she gave me a copy of what she had written so far, and I made some suggestions and gave the text a few touches of editorial grooming. In due course the book was published at her own expense, but then was accepted by a regular publisher and came out in various languages. She has also made a number of beautiful recordings of herself chanting and singing runic invocations, passages from the *Edda* and the like. Some of these were made in collaboration with David Tibet of Current 93 and Ian Read of Sol Invictus and Fire and Ice, both of whom I knew when they frequented the Enclave in Tufnell Park. At the time when I knew Freya in London and Oxford I did not foresee the international fame that she would later attain as an expert on the runes and the Nordic tradition. At the time of writing she lives in southern

Spain and continues to teach, lecture, and write about the Northern mysteries.

At the end of our stay we had a visit from three old friends, Hilmar, Lionel, and Bob Gilbert, who breezed into Oxford together. I had just passed the oral examination for my doctorate, and Hilmar greeted me with "What's up, Doc?" I photographed them in front the Old Gatehouse pub next to our house after we had lunched there.

Meanwhile Katherine, who was used to the vibrant energy of New York City, became even more frustrated with Oxford than I. She also wanted to study for a doctorate and approached the faculty of theology at Christ Church, but they turned down her application,

Fig. 5.2. Hilmar Örn Hilmarsson (*left*), Lionel Snell (*center*), and Bob Gilbert (*right*) outside the Old Gatehouse pub, Oxford, 1989.

PHOTOGRAPH BY THE AUTHOR

Fig. 5.3. Punting on the river Cherwell, Oxford,
with Freya Aswynn as passenger, circa 1987.

PHOTOGRAPH FROM THE AUTHOR'S COLLECTION

stating that the interdisciplinary nature of her studies at Harvard did not sufficiently prepare her for doctoral work. This left her feeling hurt and perplexed. She found some relief from Oxford by going on Sundays into London to attend the service at St. James's in Piccadilly, a beautiful Christopher Wren Anglican church that had a reputation for being very progressive and open-minded. The vicar was Donald Reeves, an intensely energetic, eloquent, and charismatic man, who led colorful, vibrant services that attracted a lively congregation, including a number of Jews, Catholics, and other people from outside the Church of England, who liked the welcoming atmosphere of St. James's. Katherine had, for many years, nurtured a strong vocation to enter the Episcopal priesthood and hoped that St. James's would help her to pave the way. Wishing to support her as best I could, I also often went there with her, and we became friendly with Donald Reeves and with many of the congregation members. It became known that Katherine wanted to become a priest, and, with Donald Reeves's invitation and encouragement, she soon had a regular place on the clergy team, coleading services, preaching, teaching, and creating new liturgies and rituals.

Realizing that having a non-Anglican husband might present an obstacle to her ordination, I decided to be baptized in the Church of England, and Donald Reeves readily agreed to perform the ceremony without more ado. But as the date for the baptism grew closer I began to have doubts. My main motive in converting was to help Katherine, but I could not, in all honesty, say that I believed in the Christian faith, although I had great affection for the Church of England and found its liturgy very beautiful. So I came to the conclusion it would be dishonest to convert and I canceled the appointment for the baptism.

Meanwhile, soon after we moved to Oxford we attended a three-day conference at Dartington Hall in Devon on "Art and the Renewal of the Sacred," the first of a series of conferences under the auspices of *Temenos* magazine, a periodical devoted to the interface between spirituality and the arts, which had been cofounded by the poet Kathleen Raine. Later it gave birth to the Temenos Academy, of which Prince (now King) Charles was a leading patron.

The conference was a seminal event in our lives. One of the speakers was Keith Critchlow, a cofounder of *Temenos*, professor at the Royal College of Art in London, and leading expert on sacred architecture and sacred geometry. Katherine got into conversation with him one evening and mentioned that she was having difficulty finding an academic institution where she could do a PhD. Keith immediately suggested that she do it at the Royal College of Art and offered to be her supervisor, and she readily agreed. As a subject she chose to do a rhetorical analysis of the sacred dimension of the work of Ian Hamilton Finlay.

Another speaker at the Temenos conference was Joscelyn Godwin, then professor of music at Colgate University in Hamilton, in upstate New York. He gave a spellbinding lecture on the singing of overtones, which involved audience participation, and which he delivered in a finely modulated voice that bespoke his years of musical education, first at Christ Church Choir School in Oxford and then at Cambridge, after which he had moved to the United States to pursue an academic career. I had met him briefly a few years earlier in London, but at this conference I got to know him well, and he later became one of my closest friends. There are certain qualities that I have always admired in him: a certain serenity and, to use a German word, *Feingeistigkeit* (refinement of spirit), as well as a total lack of self-importance despite his enormous erudition. The term "Renaissance man" is often misused, but Joscelyn really is one, as you can see from the extraordinary range of subjects he has written about in his books. These include *Harmonies of Heaven and Earth*, a beautiful work on the sacred in music, as well as books on the mystery cults of the ancient world, the Hermetic Brotherhood of Luxor, the mystique of the North and South Poles, the Theosophical Enlightenment and—one close to my heart—*The Pagan Dream of the Renaissance*. We have also collaborated on a *Rosicrucian Trilogy*, containing translations of the three Rosicrucian manifestos. Over the years he has been a companion in many fascinating and convivial conversations in different places: Oxford, London, Paris, Prague, Florence, and New York, among others.

After the *Temenos* conference it was back to our studies, Katherine traveling periodically to London for tutorials with Keith. Her thesis would eventually be successfully submitted under the title: "Ground of Meaning: Sacred and rhetorical dimensions in Ian Hamilton Finlay's garden landscape, Stonypath-Little Sparta." On one occasion Keith and his wife, Gail, came to Oxford at a time when Joscelyn Godwin was also visiting, and we all had a congenial picnic

Fig. 5.4. Picnicking in Christ Church Meadow, Oxford, circa 1988.
Left to right: Katherine Kurs, Joscelyn Godwin, Gail Critchlow,
Keith Critchlow, Janet Godwin.

PHOTOGRAPH BY THE AUTHOR

together in Christ Church meadow. Keith, who died in 2020, was a remarkable scholar with a profound knowledge of many things from Islamic architecture to the sacred geometry of megalithic sites. His work has helped to correct the misconception that the prehistoric inhabitants of northern Europe were primitive barbarians, when in fact their megalithic remains show that they had an advanced culture even before the Egyptian pyramids were built.

I continued the to-ing and fro-ing between my studies at Oxford and the job in London. One of the projects I became involved in at Mitchell Beazley was to create a sort of elite travel book called the *Gold Guide to Europe*. The idea (which sadly never saw publication) was to describe the five-star aspects of all the major European cities.

I was asked if I would like to write one of the entries, and I chose Vienna, as it would enable me to combine the trip with research for my thesis, and in any case Vienna was one of my favorite cities.

We flew to Vienna in the spring of 1987 and took a room in a spacious old flat in the Schleifmühlgasse owned by a pleasant couple called Hilde and Otto Wolf. We spent a couple of weeks there, working hard collecting information for the *Gold Guide* but having fun at the same time, eating in choice restaurants (often courtesy of the house) and visiting museums, galleries, and expensive shops. Vienna had held a magic for me ever since I had seen the film *The Third Man* with its opening line spoken by Trevor Howard: "I never knew the old Vienna before the war with its Strauss waltzes and its easy charm." In 1987 it still had those things—or had managed to recover them after the devastation of the war and the gloom of the postwar years. One balmy evening we wandered into the main park of the city, the Stadtpark, where a throng of people was listening to an orchestra in a little pavilion. We sat on a bench and listened entranced to some old Viennese favorites: "Wine, Women and Song," "The Blue Danube," "The Radetzky March." The "old Vienna" worked its magic on both of us, and in between our information gathering for the guide I found time to do research in the National Library for my thesis.

From Vienna we made a side trip to Prague—another city that had long held magical associations for me, especially after reading the compelling occult novels of Gustav Meyrink, a writer of the late nineteenth and early twentieth centuries, whose best known novel is *The Golem.* In esoteric Jewish tradition a golem is an artificial man, made out of clay and animated by magic. One such golem was said to have been created by the famous sixteenth-century Rabbi Loew, and there are many Jewish tales and legends about the golem as well as a series of three silent films that are considered classics of the German expressionist cinema.

We stayed in a hotel on Wenceslas Square and explored the town for two days, climbing up to the Cathedral of St. Vitus, seeing the Street of the Alchemists, which features in Meyrink's novel, taking shelter from a downpour by the Charles Bridge, and going to the Old New Synagogue and its cemetery with the grave of Rabbi Loew. Apparently, as Katherine recalls, I was so fascinated by the cemetery, the weather-worn graves and the little piles of stones left reverentially on the tombstone of the legendary rabbi, that I didn't notice when it was closing time, and we were nearly locked in.

Little did we know that two and a half years later the communist regime would collapse, but at that time the dead hand of communism was apparent everywhere in Prague. The whole town looked as though it had been put up for sale or had been suffering from planning blight for about twenty years. There was hardly a building that didn't need a coat of paint or some repairs. All of the fixtures and fittings like doorknobs, bells, signs, ashtrays, and light fittings were cheap-looking and usually in need of replacement. Everything had a makeshift, cobbled-together look. We walked around the Old Town and found it like a ghost town, the essential beauty of the buildings covered by a pall of neglect and a feeling of tired hopelessness. Something that struck me particularly were the pitiful attempts to give an impression of quality. The hotel restaurant looked superficially like a rather pretentious restaurant in the West, with a pianist in a toupee and dinner-jacketed waiters flourishing menus as though they were offering the finest cuisine in Europe, when in fact the meal we were served was revolting beyond belief.

It was a pretty bad advertisement for communism, but I couldn't help feeling that it could have worked if they had done it a bit differently and created, say, the kind of setting that William Morris describes in his utopian novel *News from Nowhere*. Morris's society is marked by a benign Arts-and-Crafts kind of socialism. It's a world where there is no private property, where the fare is simple but wholesome, the clothes plain but of good, honest cloth, the dwellings sparingly but decently furnished, and where the narrator comes across a group of road-menders looking like "a boating party at Oxford . . . handsome clean-built fellows . . . laughing and talking merrily."[1] I could imagine life in such a society being rather like a permanent retreat in a monastery, where one would live a frugal and simple but wholesome and meaningful life, with a sense of being part of a community of people with a shared vision. Possibly some of the utopian communities in the early days of the United States, such as the Pietist Ephrata Community in Pennsylvania, came close to this ideal, but certainly Prague in 1987 was light-years away from it.

From Prague we went to Munich for about four days, where I had a meeting with Ludwig Hammermayer, a professor of history at the university, who later became a good friend. Then we went on to Salzburg, where we did more research for the *Gold Guide* and I found some useful material for my thesis in the Salzburg Provincial Archive. One day we took the train over to Innsbruck where I did more research in the Tyrol Provincial Archive and, by a piece of good fortune, was able to have a meeting with Professor Helmut Reinalter at the University of Innsbruck, an expert on the history of Freemasonry, who gave me a priceless piece of information by telling me about a collection of papers in the library of the Grand Lodge of the Netherlands, relating to the Golden and Rosy Cross Order. That collection proved to be a cornerstone of my thesis, and I might never have found out about it had I not met Professor Reinalter.

Toward the end of the summer I heard that I had been awarded a substantial grant from the British Academy that would enable me to leave Mitchell Beazley and concentrate on my studies, so at the at the age of forty-four I started the autumn term of 1987 as a full-time graduate student. At the same time my younger son, Jason, took up a place to read mathematics at Oriel College right next to Christ Church. It was an odd situation having a father and son both studying at Oxford at the same time, but it never bothered us, and we saw a lot of each other. Jason came for meals to Christ Church or to our flat, and we went for walks and played tennis at the Christ Church sports ground. Meanwhile my elder son, Angus, was majoring in physics at Edinburgh University.

In October came a new step on my spiritual path. Unexpectedly we had to go to New York to find a new tenant for Katherine's apartment on West End Avenue. Katherine's building was just around the corner from the B'nai Jeshurun synagogue. Our visit extended over a weekend, and on Saturday morning I attended a service in the synagogue, mainly out of curiosity as I had never been to a Jewish service before. I was given a prayer shawl as I entered, and later a friendly man came up and handed me a yarmulke, a small white skullcap. The interior was very ornate in a warm sort of way, with much stained glass and walls covered with intricate patterns in green, brown, and gold. The singing was beautiful, and there came a moving moment when the Torah scroll was carried around the temple, allowing the congregation to touch it with their prayer books or shawls. I held back, as I was unsure whether, as a non-Jew, I would be entitled to touch the scroll. When it came to the sermon, the rabbi, a young man, who I later learned was from Argentina, spoke of the significance of the day, Shabbat Shuvah. After speaking for a while he invited members of the congregation to give their comments, and a microphone was handed round. Many people spoke eloquently about what guilt means, what its value is, and how we can deal with it and learn not to repeat our errors. I found it all very moving. That was the beginning for me of a flirtation with Judaism and very nearly a conversion, of which more anon.

The spring of the following year, 1988, was marked by tragedy. On May 1, my mother died suddenly and unexpectedly of an attack of viral pneumonia, which came out of the blue. Katherine and I were in Paris working on a new edition of my guidebook to the city when we received the news. We flew immediately to Edinburgh for the funeral and the burial at the Grange Cemetery at a lovely spot with a view toward Arthur's Seat. For me it was a painful farewell, as there were issues from the past that I should have discussed with her and tried to resolve, mainly connected with the trauma of "Pritchard's" school and my consequent emotional withdrawal, which prevented me from having the kind of warm, natural relationship that one should have with one's parents. I have learned that one should say the things that need to be said before it's too late, even though it's more comfortable to let sleeping dogs lie. Four months later my father married Karina Williamson and remained happily married to her until his death in 2005.

The first few months of the following year, 1989, were dominated by final work on our doctoral theses, but one pleasant interruption was when the writer and filmmaker Tobias Churton asked us to take part in a documentary film on the Rosicrucian movement, which he was making for the Dutch businessman and Maecenas, Joost Ritman, founder of the now famous Ritman Library in Amsterdam. I was interviewed speaking about the Gnostic features of Rosicrucianism. Katherine and a man called Bob were filmed holding up a glass chalice with wine pouring out of the sky to represent the gnosis— an effect achieved with a watering can. It was the start of a lasting friendship with Tobias.

In the summer term I submitted my doctoral thesis under the title "The Rosicrucian Revival and the German Counter-Enlightenment" and was duly awarded the title of DPhil—it would later be published by Brill of Leiden under the title *The Rose Cross and the Age of Reason*. The final hurdle was the oral examination, which took place at the Examination Schools on the High Street. I waited nervously in the entrance hall until I was summoned by a bell ringing somewhere in the depths of the building and made my way to a small room where my examiners, David Sorkin and Tim Blanning, were waiting. After

Fig. 5.5. London friends at a farewell dinner before our
departure for America in 1989. Clockwise from *bottom left*:
Jessica Johnson, Jean Morton-Williams, Jeffrey Somers,
Nobuko Somers, Jeremy Cranswick, Katherine Kurs, Zachary Cox.

PHOTOGRAPH BY THE AUTHOR

some tough questioning they declared my thesis accepted. And so, at the age of forty-five, I walked out onto the High Street having attainted the title of DPhil. On the same day Katherine was awarded her doctorate from the Royal College of Art for her thesis on Ian Hamilton Finlay.

We shipped a load of books and other possessions off to New York and booked our flights. Shortly before leaving we held a farewell dinner for our London friends at an Indian restaurant near Euston station. In August we boarded a plane for New York to start a new phase of our life together in the city where both my mother and Katherine had grown up.

6

Life in the Big Apple

We moved into Katherine's two-room apartment on West End Avenue on the Upper West Side of Manhattan, in a building with a marquee over the entrance and a uniformed doorman ("Have a nice day, Mr. McIntosh!"). After settling in I began looking for work. University posts for the coming academic year were already filled, so I would have to find an interim job. I began treading the crowded, sunbaked sidewalks of Manhattan, buoyed by the energy of the city but only half believing that I was really there. This was the city where my mother grew up and which she had always loved. Something of her optimism and go-getting quality must have sustained me as I walked those streets. My mood matched the words of the Frank Sinatra song:

> *If I can make it here I can make it anywhere.*
> *It's up to you, New York, New York.*

I signed on with employment agencies, went for interviews with a variety of firms, even took typing tests—I was prepared to do practically any kind of work. Then I had an amazingly lucky break. I called my friends and former hosts Lisa Ritchie and Clyde Farnsworth in Washington to ask for their advice and they suggested that I contact their friend Russell Boner, who ran the Division of Information (DOI) at the United Nations Development Programme (UNDP), which occupied a building on First Avenue opposite the main UN complex. I went for an interview and a few days later I was offered a job as one of their roving journalists, reporting on economic development projects in the Third World for the various magazines that the division published. It seemed as though, by the wave of a magic wand, I had been whisked from a hand-to-mouth existence as an Oxford graduate student to a prestigious job in a key part of the United Nations system. I had an office to myself on the nineteenth floor of the UNDP building with a dramatic view. Along the opposite side of the avenue I could see a row of flagpoles flying the flags of the member nations of the UN. Beyond it was the towering slab of the UN Secretariat building, flanked by the long, white structure, shaped like an ocean liner, that housed the General Assembly chamber. All around were the skyscrapers of the East Side, and in the gaps between them I could look across the East River to Long Island.

My first assignment was to go to the Ivory Coast in West Africa to report on a diamond-cutting venture and a fish farming project. It was the start of a period during which I traveled all over the world for UNDP and later for the United Nations Educational, Scientific and Cultural Organization (UNESCO). My work took me to, among other places, Venezuela, Turkey, Tunisia, eastern Europe, India, South Korea, Australia, South Africa, Botswana, and Mozambique.

The United Nations was a marvelous place to work—a city within a city, with all kinds of facilities including a superb language school where I signed up for a course in Russian. Having learned a bit of the language during my semester at Columbia, I was able to skip the beginners' level, and over the next three years or so I acquired a reasonable speaking and reading competence. At a showing of a

Fig. 6.1. Working as an information officer with the United Nations Development Programme, 1989.
PHOTOGRAPH FROM THE AUTHOR'S COLLECTION

Russian film at the UN I met a beautiful Russian pianist called Vera with whom I had a marvelous love affair—by then Katherine and I had separated for reasons that I shall explain shortly.

During that period I also visited Russia for the first time. Katherine put me in touch with an Episcopal priest who was planning a trip there with a group of born-again Christians eager to see firsthand how Christianity was reviving after the suppression of the communist years. Rather to my surprise, I found them most likeable and interesting people, especially one called Frank, formerly the leader of a criminal gang, who had been caught and sentenced to a long prison term. Having been converted by the prison chaplain, he served a reduced sentence and became ordained in the Episcopal Church. As a fine example of poacher turned gamekeeper, he went into the prison service. By that time some prisons had been privatized, and he ended up managing two private prisons as well as ministering to the spiritual needs of the inmates and helping to prepare them for reintegration into civilian life.

When we landed in St. Petersburg it was April, and the weather was still cold and wintry, which lent a kind of wistful beauty to the city. Looking back, there are certain things that stand out in my mind from that trip: traveling in the airport bus down Moskovsky Prospect with its endless phalanx of buildings in the heavy, Stalinist neoclassical style; having supper with a Russian family—mother, son, and daughter—in their cozy apartment in a rather grim tower block in the suburbs; visiting the exquisite, wedding-cake palace of Pushkin and hearing the music of a military brass band floating out over the snow-covered park; and of course exploring the riches of the Hermitage Museum and marveling at the beauty of the main city with its canals and its terraces of mansions and palaces stretching to infinity. We flew on to Moscow—to the Kremlin Museum, Red Square, Lenin's tomb, the Bolshoi Ballet, and more. I bought a model of St. Basil's Cathedral to take home as a souvenir. Russia changes you. I developed a profound love of the country, which has remained with me.

In the course of my fifteen years or so working for the UN system I had certain experiences and came to certain conclusions that had a bearing on my path toward paganism. I soon became aware of a tension within the UN and indeed within the whole endeavor that one might call the global project. This project is founded on a paradigm that stems from the European Enlightenment of the seventeenth and eighteenth centuries—a universalist paradigm of democracy, equality, human rights, freedom, justice, and progress. This is all very laudable, but it inevitably comes into conflict with a different paradigm that is particularist rather than universal, whose watchwords are "diversity," "multiculturalism," and "the right of cultures to their own norms." In the area of human rights, for example, a crucial question is whether those rights are individual or collective. When you take a culture of collective rights and try to integrate it within a culture of individual rights—or vice versa—a conflict is bound to happen.

A typical manifestation of this dilemma happened a few years ago in Germany when there was a campaign to ban the circumcision of infant males. The campaigners argued that the practice was an infringement of the rights of the child since it involved a physical mutilation that could have consequences later on for sexual functioning—interestingly, one of the supporters of the ban was a man from Israel. Immediately there was an outcry from the traditional Jewish establishment that such a ban would be an attack on religious freedom. In the end the issue was effectively swept under the carpet, and the practice was allowed to continue. Basically, the government did not want to face up to the essential issue: the rights of the individual versus the rights of a community to their traditional practices. Time and time again I have seen people in the global project getting themselves into a twist when confronted by this dilemma. I have talked to people who would defend the practice of male circumcision but draw the line at female genital mutilation. So in effect they end up saying: "Of course all societies have the right to their own norms . . . except when I don't like them." There is an insoluble dilemma here. If I opt for the global model it will inevitably lead to the erosion of local norms and traditions. On the other hand, if I stand up for local, time-honored practices at all costs, I will sooner or later be confronted with things that I find deeply abhorrent, such as female genital mutilation.

The notion of progress—another shibboleth of the global agenda—also gives rise to contradictory positions, often within the same individual. Let's take, for example, the case of a traditional community such as the Bushmen of the Kalahari Desert in Africa. As Laurens van der Post shows in his beautiful book *The Lost World of the Kalahari*, the Bushmen are a unique tribe with a unique way of life. Evidently they originally came from somewhere outside of Africa, as they have somewhat Asian-appearing features and lighter skins. They are small in stature and live in what development experts would call total poverty. They have very few possessions and survive only from what they can hunt and gather in the desert. Their life expectancy is commensurately low. At the same time they have a rich oral tradition and can recite endless myths and sagas about their community, handed down over countless generations. Their customs and ceremonies are finely grained, as witness the elaborate courtship conventions that they observe. In recent decades this unique community has been subjected to near genocide, driven out of their ancestral lands to make way for diamond mining and tourism, and resettled under conditions completely alien to them.

If you confronted a development worker with this case they would probably twist and turn and finally argue that the resettled Bushmen have a much higher standard of living than they had before, and that after all progress always has its price. But then what about the right of communities to their own norms and way of life? Are they to be swept aside whenever they conflict with what the industrialized world calls progress? Or is it perhaps time to question our notion of progress itself? Ultimately the global model of progress is a one-size-fits-all model, which admittedly has its advantages: for example, the whole world observes international times zones, telephone codes, air traffic conventions, and the like. But at the same time global progress means the disappearance of many local and Indigenous languages along with the inherited knowledge that is enshrined in them. There is a popular slogan around the UN that says: "Think global, act local. And think local, act global." A fine-sounding motto, but is it in fact an attempt to square the circle?

In one of the UN buildings close to my office there was an interfaith chapel, which in fact appeared to be primarily for Christians,

Jews, and Muslims. The interior was stark and minimalistic except for the symbols of the three religions—a cross, a Star of David, and a crescent and five-pointed star—displayed on one wall. The concept was well meant, but the place was absolutely devoid of any spiritual energy or atmosphere. It was like the religious equivalent of Esperanto, which tries to be an "everywhere" language and ends up being a "nowhere" one. Or, to make another comparison, it was like one of those composite faces made up of photographs of thousands of people from all over the world, resulting in a face without character or soul. It brought home to me that the quality of soul is something that needs a nourishing soil in order to flourish, in other words a "somewhere." As I traveled around the world I found this quality of "somewhere" concentrated in all places where there was an authentic, organic culture. I found it in the mountainous areas of Korea, in Holy Russia, in the Zen gardens of Kyoto, and in Iceland, among other places.

Soon after I started at the United Nations there came the collapse of communism, the disintegration of the Soviet Union, and the fall of the Berlin Wall, with people on the New York streets offering "fresh wall for sale." In the wake of these events came a tidal wave of triumphalist capitalism that I found distasteful. I encountered an example of this in Budapest where I attended the ceremonial reopening of the stock exchange, which had been closed since just after the Second World War. One of the speakers at the ceremony was a representative of the United States Securities and Exchange Commission, who asserted that we no longer need to lie awake wondering what the best economic system is because we know that it is the Western capitalist model. Really? Well, admittedly communism was not the ideal system, but laissez-faire capitalism is beset by serious problems of its own, and perhaps it is time to look for a different paradigm altogether.

Often I could combine my trips with a stopover in Britain,

and on a visit to London I had one of those strange meetings with Hilmar, whom I had not seen for several years. I was on a bus traveling up Charing Cross Road when I had an impulse to get off the bus and go to a café in Soho that had earlier been a haunt of mine. I walked into the café and there was Hilmar sitting at a table with an Icelandic woman, his then partner. We had some pleasant meetings and meals over the next few days together with my Russian girlfriend, Vera, who was visiting London with me. Then somehow I lost touch with Hilmar again for a while.

Between these trips my life in New York continued. So did my spiritual quest. Not yet ready for paganism, I leaned for a time toward Judaism. Feeling the need for some kind of spiritual life, I began to go regularly to services in the B'nai Jeshurun synagogue. There was something warm and enveloping about the atmosphere there, and also something feminine, despite the patriarchal deity that they worshipped. For me the most beautiful moment in the Friday evening service was the arrival of the invisible Sabbath Bride, when the congregation turned to the door to greet her. After a while Katherine started going with me and we soon became friendly with the two rabbis and with various members of the congregation. In this experience Katherine was for the first time acknowledging and exploring her Jewish roots and ancestry, although she was still intent on being ordained as a priest in the Episcopal Church. Having Gemini as her sun sign, she had no difficulty in going to the synagogue on Friday evening or Saturday morning and then to the Episcopal Cathedral of St. John the Divine on Sunday, as she struggled through the obstacle course of the selection process for ordination, which involved endless interviews and psychological tests. A couple of times she came close to her goal, only to be rejected and sent back to the beginning of the whole process. It was like something out of a Kafka novel and I grew increasingly angry at the mean and shabby way she was treated. Sometimes I went with her to the church out of solidarity, but as time went on I could not pretend that I was happy about her wishing to be ordained in an institution that could treat her in such a way, and consequently she felt let down by me. Cracks began to appear in our relationship.

Meanwhile we continued attending the synagogue, and I began seriously to think about conversion. The services moved me in a way that I had not experienced in any Christian church. In fairness I have to say that B'nai Jeshurun was extremely unusual in its warmth, vitality, and friendliness, in the intelligent, thought-provoking quality of the addresses and discussions, and in the beautiful music, which often set the worshippers dancing joyfully around the synagogue in a circle. Katherine encouraged me as my urge to convert grew stronger, but, as the moment for my formal conversion approached, I drew back, as I had done in the case of my near conversion to the Church of England. Appealing though Anglicanism and Judaism were, they were not where my roots lay.

Paradoxically it was the rabbi of the synagogue who unwittingly helped to push me in the direction of paganism. One evening I attended a lecture by him in which he spoke about the difference between the monotheistic and the pagan religions. In the former, he said, human history proceeds in a straight line toward some goal, be it the Last Judgment, the coming of the Messiah, or whatever, whereas in paganism everything goes in a great circle. And in that moment I realized in a flash that I was a man of the circle, or perhaps the spiral, and not the straight line. Later I learned that the rabbi's observation was an oversimplification, but never mind. It was a key moment for me nevertheless. My sojourn in New York was also important in another way for my pagan path. Sometimes we have to step away for a while from the place where we belong in order to realize that it is indeed where we belong. From the vantage point of America I looked back across the Atlantic and realized that I was a north European and that the ancient gods of northern

Europe were my gods. This realization also contributed to my decision not to convert to Judaism.

For Katherine, my decision was a big disappointment. What with that and my failure to give her sufficient moral support in her ordination struggle, the rift between us was growing wider. It was further compounded by the realization that we had diametrically opposite views on certain important issues. Nevertheless, when our separation and divorce came, we remained very close friends and still are. Meanwhile it was becoming clear that, for budgetary reasons, my job at the United Nations was not going to be made permanent. I began to set my sights on a return to England.

During the last year of my sojourn in New York I became involved in another relationship. My then partner, Deborah, was a practitioner of a form of therapy using the breath, which she persuaded me to try. It involved lying down and hyperventilating in a certain way, the idea being to release knots of emotional and physical tension or blockage. I lay down on a couch while she sat beside me and monitored the proceedings. I forget whether it was at the first or second session that I had a dramatic breakthrough. I lay there hyperventilating, and for several minutes nothing unusual happened. Then I began to have the feeling that something was building up inside me, ready to burst out. I took a few more breaths and suddenly heard myself give a deafening roar like that of an angry caveman or gorilla. I felt possessed by some immensely powerful entity, yet at the same time my normal self was observing what was going on. Afterward I had a sense of calmness and release, as though I had given expression to a long-suppressed part of myself. Soon afterward we held another session and the same thing happened. Seeking a name for the entity or sub-personality that had come through, I hit for some reason on the name of Odoacer, the ferocious fifth-century Germanic chieftain who made himself King of Italy. I realized that he was an expression of long pent-up anger inside me, which very occasionally came to the surface in a violent outburst of temper. Now I resolved that, when anger was called for, I would let Odoacer speak, but without overreacting.

The opportunity soon came to put this to the test. At that time I was editor of a magazine published by the United Nations Development Programme. The unit for which I worked was headed by an African with whom I got on reasonably well most of the time, but who could sometimes be rather high-handed. One day he called me on my office phone and berated me for having sent an incorrect message to one of our offices in Africa—a very minor error of no real consequence. I told him I was doing the best job I could and I didn't like his attitude. There was a stunned silence, then I heard him say: "What!?" I repeated what I had said. Another stunned silence, then he said: "You'd better come in." So I walked into his office with Odoacer at my side, to find the boss sitting behind his desk, pointing an accusing finger at me and saying: "Now look here . . ." Then the conversation went like this:

Me, pointing a finger back and saying in an angry voice: "No, you look here!"

Boss, startled: "Are you all right?"

Me: "Yes, I'm all right, but I'm in a very irascible mood."

Boss: "What are you going to do, hit me?"

At which I nearly laughed. Suddenly the tension was defused and we were able to have a friendly discussion. Since then I have tried to react in the same way in similar situations, but admittedly not always successfully. An angry barbarian chieftain can sometimes get out of control.

During my time at the United Nations I interviewed many impressive and fascinating people. Two of them stand out in my mind particularly. One was the Bangladeshi economist Professor Mohammed Yunus, founder of the Grameen Bank, a microcredit initiative that assists mini-enterprises and has lifted thousands of

Fig. 6.2. Interviewing Julius Nyerere, former president of Tanzania, at the United Nations, New York, in about 1992.

PHOTOGRAPH FROM THE AUTHOR'S COLLECTION

people, mainly women, out of dire poverty. The other was the ex-president of Tanzania, Julius Nyerere, who had led his country into independence. Affectionately known in Tanzania as Mwalimu (Swahili for "teacher"), he had his own vision of a form of African socialism, which he saw essentially as a continuation of African tribal traditions. While some of his policies were controversial there is no doubt that he was devoted above all to the welfare of his people. I found him extremely friendly and approachable, and I feel honored to have met him.

7

Experiencing Sacred Space

Traveling around the world on United Nations business I found time to visit places of special numinosity—sacred natural sites, shrines, temples, and gardens. On a visit to India in 1990 I caught a glimpse of the Hindu pantheon, which consists of innumerable gods, goddesses, and devas under an overarching supreme deity. In Delhi I visited the beautiful Laxminarayan Temple, built in the 1930s by a rich industrialist and dedicated to Lakshmi, goddess of prosperity, and Laxminarayan, another name for Vishnu, the Preserver. The temple also has shrines to Shiva, Ganesha, the monkey god Hanuman, and, in interfaith spirit, Lord Buddha. A friendly priest daubed a spot of color on my forehead and hung a garland of flowers around my neck.

In Delhi I also visited the garden of the Red Fort, created by the Mughal emperor Shah Jahan. Once famed as one of the most magnificent gardens of India, it is now somewhat run to seed, but the essential features of a traditional Islamic garden are still there—the shady pavilions and colonnades, the central pool, and the four water channels representing the four rivers of paradise. Shah Jahan's more famous monument is the Taj Mahal, which I visited on a day trip, marveling at the great, shimmering, white mausoleum with its domes and minarets, facing a garden laid out in the familiar Islamic pattern.

Another place that stands out in my memory is South Korea, which I visited twice. In addition to Buddhism, Christianity, and various other religions, Korea has a deeply rooted pagan tradition. Paganism in Korea is bound up with a strong tradition of shamanism, which coexists very happily with Buddhism but is often at odds with the more zealous of the Christian community. Central to Korean shamanism is the interaction with nature spirits, most importantly the group of mountain spirits known as San-shin.[1] Mountains cover 75 percent of the country's territory and are traditionally revered by the Koreans, as shown by the stone cairns that abound on the slopes and beside mountain paths. When passing a cairn, the respectful traveler will add a stone as a mark of homage to the San-shin. Villages also have their tutelary San-shin, and collectively the San-shin form the guardian spirit of the country as a whole. The typical San-shin is portrayed as a wise old man holding a knobbly staff, with a tiger crouching beside him. Shrines to San-shin, containing this image, are often found within the grounds of Buddhist monasteries, which shows how the two religions live happily side by side. I found it moving how the Koreans have such an intimate relationship with the spirits of the land. In this way Korea reminded me of Iceland with its tradition of elves and nature spirits. And the old man with his knobbly staff and tiger is reminiscent of Odin with his staff and his wolves.

A special highlight of my second visit to Korea was going on a bus tour to a sort of living reconstruction of a traditional Korean folk village, where shamanism was very much in evidence. At the entrance were "guardian stones" dangling on pieces of string for visitors to touch and make a wish. Inside the village compound I was just in time to see a wonderful dancing and drumming performance by men in brightly colored costumes, some with colored balls on their hats, others with caps trailing white ribbons that whirled as they danced. I was told that this was a so-called farmers' dance to promote fertility of the land. In one house I glimpsed an altar with three gilded Buddhas side by side. This was the abode of a female shaman who would tell your fortune for a fee.

In the courtyard of another house I witnessed part of a traditional wedding ceremony conducted by two priests or shamans in white costumes and tall black hats. The bridegroom arrived first with his best man. Then came the bride in an ornate costume and a very heavy-looking headdress, flanked by her two bridesmaids. On an altar were candles, piles of fruit, and two live chickens, tied up—later I was told that they were released at a certain point in the ceremony. I realized that the whole village was a creation for the benefit of the visitors, but I still found it impressive. At the entrance to some of the houses was a picture of a tiger smoking a long pipe—a reference to the traditional Korean way of beginning a story, which is to say "when the tiger smoked" instead of "once upon a time."

Also memorable was the Palace of Shining Happiness in Seoul. The grounds of the palace include the Secret Garden with a lotus pond overlooked by the Jahamnu Pavilion, built in 1776 by the enlightened ruler King Jeongjo. A notice informed me: "The name of the building means cosmic accord. It was aimed at being a place where scholars could contemplate universal principles, cultivate their character in accordance with the ways of heaven and prepare to govern the nation properly." A noble concept, reminiscent of the guardians of Plato's *Republic*, and one that the modern world could profitably emulate.

In the palace grounds I photographed one of the ubiquitous fertility figures known as *dol hareubangs*, characterized by their phallus-shaped heads. These belong to the Korean form of geomancy, that is to say the science of working with earth energies, and they are ubiquitous in the rural parts of the country. They have their

Fig. 7.1. A *dol hareubang* (spirit of fertility) in the grounds
of the Palace of Shining Happiness, Seoul.
See also color plate 2.

PHOTOGRAPH BY THE AUTHOR

counterparts in the herms of Greek tradition, stone pillars typically
with the bearded head of Hermes (god of travelers as well as scribes,
merchants, and thieves) at the top and an erect phallus protruding
from lower down. In both cases these objects are believed to influence the flow of subtle energies through the ground.

After my first visit to Korea I had an equally memorable visit to Japan. Together with Masakazu Yoshimura, the Japanese translator of my book on the Rosicrucians, I took a tour of the Zen Buddhist gardens and temples in the city. The first one we came to was the Tenryu-ji (*ji* meaning temple), where the garden had a little lake with islands, mossy banks, rocks, and trees, all flowing together in apparently effortless harmony—deceptively, because in fact the whole effect was the result of enormous effort and care. The position of every rock was deliberately chosen, and the velvety moss covering the ground had to be constantly weeded by the monks, who treated the task as a spiritual exercise, plucking the weeds and at the same time symbolically removing the impurities from themselves. We moved on to another temple, the Ryoan-ji, famous for its sand garden, and then to the Daitoku-ji, where we were served a kind of vegetarian sushi lunch. While we were eating, a jolly, shaven-headed monk announced that, as an English guest was present, he would like to sing an English song. He then proceeded to sing a completely garbled version of "She'll Be Coming Round the Mountain When She Comes," which included the lines: "She'll be eating vegetarian food when she comes" and "She'll be doing a labor of love when she comes."

In one of the Kyoto gardens I paused by a lake to take a photograph, and in that moment a white crane, symbol of longevity and good fortune in the Japanese tradition, landed on a rock and stood there as though posing for the picture. It was the kind of instant that might have been captured in a *haiku*—a combination of a magical moment and a magical place. Since then I have thought of cranes, storks, and herons as being my totem creatures.

It is one of the great deprivations in the modern world, especially in the industrialized West, that sacred places have become so diminished. Even the concept of a sacred place is lacking in the prevailing secular culture of modernity, although there remains a deep human need for such places, as witness the large numbers of people in many countries who flock at certain times of year to prehistoric sites of power such as Stonehenge in England, the Externsteine in Germany, or Arkaim in Russia. It is fortunate that these famous sites have been preserved, but in pagan times there was an infinitely greater abundance of such sites: not only temples and megaliths, but sacred places and things in nature—groves, springs, mountains, caves, and lakes. These were typically places for public gatherings and rituals, but there were also private sacred spaces, like the household shrine, the altar to a protective deity, or the niche for the ancestors—places that bring enchantment into everyday life. Certainly the monotheistic religions have their sacred places, where enchantment can be found, but it is enchantment of a different kind from that of the pagan world, with its innumerable deities and nature spirits.

My own pagan journey has been bound up with my attraction toward sacred places. I was lucky to grow up in Britain, which is unusually rich in ancient sites steeped in lore and legend—places like Stonehenge, the Rollright Stones, the Callanish Stones in the Hebrides, and Glastonbury in the West Country, associated with the Grail legends and the Archangel Michael, ostensibly a Christian figure but in fact an ancient solar deity. There's also the beautiful eighteenth-century park of Stourhead in Wiltshire, evoking the journey of Aeneas in Virgil's *Aeneid*, the estate of Stowe in Buckinghamshire with its statues of the ancient Anglo-Saxon gods, and of course Ian Hamilton Finlay's Little Sparta, dedicated to Apollo, which had such a profound influence on my journey. Traveling further afield, I marveled at the Versailles park, built for the ultra-Catholic monarch Louis XIV but filled with a multitude of pagan gods, presided over by Apollo, symbolizing the Sun King himself. In Italy I explored more gardens filled with pagan deities: the Villa d'Este near Rome, the Boboli Garden in Florence, the Villa Garzoni at Collodi, and the enchanting Tarot Garden in the Latium, created by Niki de Saint Phalle.

In Germany I found a surprising abundance of wonderful symbol-filled gardens, such as the eighteenth-century park of Wörlitz in Saxony-Anhalt, built around a salient of the river Elbe, which takes the visitor on an initiatory journey via waterways, tunnels, grottos, temples, statues, and labyrinthine paths. Roughly contemporary with Wörlitz is the park at Louisenlund in Schleswig-Holstein, built by Prince Carl von Hessen-Kassel, a Rosicrucian, alchemist, and prominent Freemason, who filled the park with symbolic features including a Freemasons' Tower, most of which sadly have since fallen into ruin. The property is now occupied by an elite boarding school. On the initiative of the headmaster, Peter Rösner, a project is underway to rebuild the tower and restore other features in the park. The project is assisted by an advisory board, of which I am a member. Another of my favorite gardens is Thieles' Garden in Bremerhaven,

Fig. 7.2. The author with a satyr in Thieles' Garden, Bremerhaven.
See also color plate 3.

PHOTOGRAPH BY DONATE MCINTOSH

created over several decades from the 1920s by Gustav and Georg Thiele and the latter's wife, Grete. Now a public park, it is a place of special enchantment, with artificial lakes, fountains, groves, meandering paths, colonnades, and numerous figures—mythical, human, and half-human. Donate, my wife (about whom I shall say more later), photographed me there sitting beside a jolly satyr with a mischievous smile and enormous ears. Gardens like these provided inspiration for the garden that Donate and I created at our home in Lower Saxony, and I described many of them in my book *Gardens of the Gods* (2005). But that was to come later. Meanwhile my restless life continued.

8

Key Encounters

In the summer of 1993 at the age of forty-nine I went back to England and moved into a flat that I had bought in the north London suburb of Crouch End. A few weeks later I went to Poland for the wedding of my younger son, Jason, to his Polish bride, Natalia, whom he had met during an internship that I had arranged for him at the UNDP office in Warsaw. Boarding a train in Warsaw to go home via Poznan and Berlin, I was robbed of my wallet, which contained my US green card. This was surely a sign from the Fates that my phase as an American "resident alien" was definitively over and that my future lay in Europe. Soon after returning to London I saw an advertisement in the *Guardian* for a job in Hamburg as head of publications at the UNESCO Institute for Education. I applied, was accepted, found a tenant for my flat, and moved to Hamburg in February of 1994.

The Institute (now called the UNESCO Institute for Lifelong Learning) is housed in a fine building that was built around 1910 as the home of the shipping magnate Albert Ballin, the main architect of the Hapag-Lloyd company. It is located in a posh district of tree-lined streets and expensive properties near the Dammtor station.

The job was extremely demanding from the start—editing a journal called the *International Review of Education*, overseeing the
publications program, and acting as public relations officer—but
my colleagues were friendly and working conditions were pleasant.
For the first couple of years I lived in an attic flat in the district of
Eimsbüttel, then moved to an apartment in the famous red light district of Sankt Pauli. It was in a quiet, cobbled street of old houses
in a picturesque enclave with a mixed population of old established
residents, young "alternative" types, immigrants, and a few pioneering yuppies. My building was opposite the Sankt Pauli church with
its quiet, leafy graveyard. On one occasion, for the purposes of a film,
the vicarage beside the church was turned into a naughty nightclub
with red lights in the windows. The area was a delightful little oasis
between the harbor and the demi-monde of the Reeperbahn—I used
to say that I lived "between the Devil and the deep blue sea."

Nearby in the vicinity of the harbor was a pub that I used to frequent called the Kapitäns Eck (Captain's Corner), where a "singing
landlady" called Ingeborg performed every Sunday morning from the
small hours through to lunchtime. In a husky voice like a German Edith
Piaf she would give lusty renderings of "Lili Marleen," "Rolling Home,"
and other songs of the Hamburg waterfront—songs with a bittersweet,
romantic quality, full of that sense of longing that is so German. It is
a longing for longing itself, as in the Marlene Dietrich song, where she
asks herself whether she should wish for happiness or sadness, for if she
found happiness she would long to be sad again. Similarly, the German
sailor dreams of faraway places with exotic names, but when he is there
he dreams of the homeland. One of those sentimental songs, a popular
hit from the 1950s, is called "Seemann, wo ist deine Heimat? "(Sailor,
where is your home?).[1] One of the verses goes:

> *Rio, Shanghai und Tahiti*
> *Brachten dir Freude und Glück,*

Doch suchst du den Haven der Liebe,
Dann kehre nach Hause zurück.

(Very freely translated: *Rio, Shanghai and Tahiti / Brought you moments of joy / Yet if you seek love's harbor / Then steer a course for home.*)

Fig. 8.1. My drawing of the Antonistrasse, Hamburg, where I lived for several years.

Fig. 8.2. With Scottish friend Rennie Johnson in
the Kapitäns Eck pub in Hamburg.
PHOTOGRAPH FROM THE AUTHOR'S COLLECTION

It was a song that somehow spoke to me. I had traveled the
world and the winds had brought me to Hamburg, but my travels
were not yet over. In my first summer at UIE I attended an educational conference in Copenhagen in my capacity as editor of the
International Review of Education. After the conference ended I was
walking down the long shopping street called Stroget, which winds
its way through the center of the city. Looking for somewhere to have
dinner, I stopped in front of a café called Krasnapolsky to read a
menu placed in the window. Suddenly a figure appeared in the doorway and a hand reached out to grasp my shoulder. It was Hilmar
Hilmarsson—and again at a café! I blurted out something about how
amazing it was, to which he replied nonchalantly: "No, it's not—we
always meet like this." I have often reflected on the phenomenon of
coincidence, which has played a big part in my life, and I once coined

the aphorism: "Coincidence is the universe thinking aloud." The psychologist Carl Gustav Jung talked a lot about "meaningful coincidence," and this second coincidental meeting with Hilmar was certainly meaningful. It turned out that he and his then-partner Gunna Sika and their small son, Odin, were living in a village on the island of Møn off the Baltic coast, where Hilmar had set up a recording studio to pursue his career as a composer, chiefly of film music. I visited Hilmar several times on the island and again after he moved to Copenhagen, by which time he had separated from Gunna Sika and married Ragna, an Icelandic artist and writer, and they had a small daughter. In due course they moved back to Iceland, but we made sure that we stayed in touch.

In the autumn of the following year—1995—came an event organized by the New York Open Center, an institution devoted to alternative spirituality and holistic learning, which had been founded by Walter Bebe, a wealthy New York lawyer, and which was run with great verve and charisma by Ralph White, an émigré from Britain who had for a time been in charge of the Findhorn Community on the east coast of Scotland. I had already given two talks at the Open Center, one on the Rosicrucian tradition and another on sacred and symbolic gardens, so I knew Ralph well. One day he telephoned me at my office and said that he was organizing a conference in the Czech Republic in honor of the late Frances Yates, to be called "The Rosicrucian Enlightenment Revisited," and would I be interested in being a presenter? I gladly agreed. It was the beginning of my involvement in a series of Open Center conferences that were to be among the highlights of my life.

The conference was held in September. I took a train from the Dammtor Station in Hamburg—a beautiful journey through Berlin, Dresden, and along part of the Elbe—arriving in the late afternoon in Prague, which I found completely transformed since my visit there in 1987. Instead of the gray, listless city that it had been in those days, it was now a free-market tourists' paradise with glossy shops selling every kind of ware, including overpriced Bohemian glass and ceramics. There were also discos, casinos, and restaurants of every variety, including McDonald's. I had the impression the place had gone a bit too far in the opposite direction after throwing off the communist yoke.

Next day I met the conference party at the airport and we were driven in a bus to Česky Krumlov, a beautiful little town on the River Moldau (Vltava in Czech), overlooked by a castle with a marvelous round tower like something out of an alchemical engraving—we later learned that it had indeed been used for alchemy. The castle had been the home of the Counts of Rožmberk, one of whom had been host to the Elizabethan magus John Dee when the latter had visited Bohemia. The town was wonderfully atmospheric, with winding, higgledy-piggledy streets and architecture ranging from medieval to baroque. Walking through part of the town I thought I had strayed into a time warp. I saw people in eighteenth-century costumes wandering about and shopping at an old-fashioned street market, and there was a mysterious-looking horse-drawn carriage with a coat of arms painted on the side. It turned out that this was all part of the set for a film of *Pinocchio* being made by the Walt Disney company.

The talks at the conference, many of them by valued friends of mine, included Nicholas Goodrick-Clarke on John Dee's mission to Bohemia, his wife Clare Goodrick-Clarke on the educationist Comenius, John Matthews on the symbolism of the Grail and the Rose, Joscelyn Godwin on "Magical Gardens and Chambers of Marvels," Warren Kenton on the Kabbalah, John Michell on divine numerology and sacred geography, and Adam McLean on the efflorescence of alchemical publishing in the late-sixteenth and early-seventeenth centuries. I gave a workshop on alchemy and a talk on Rosicrucianism as the last presentation. During the conference some of the speakers and participants performed a short play based on part of Gustav Meyrink's novel *The Angel of the Western Window*, set partly in the Elizabethan era. Nicholas Goodrick-Clarke directed the play, and the actors included Thomas Hakl as John Dee and Jay Kinney as the emperor Rudolf II.

Among the conference guests were the publisher Donald Weiser and his wife, Betty Lundsted. As my book *The Rosy Cross Unveiled* was by then out of print, I asked Donald if he could publish a new edition, which he later agreed to do. Another guest for part of the conference was Vladislav Zadrobilek, who had run a samizdat operation producing esoteric books during the communist days and now had a regular publishing firm and a bookshop in Prague. A meeting with him in Prague was arranged by Michal Pober, a Czech by birth

Fig. 8.3. Performance of a play based on Gustav Meyrink's novel *The Angel of the Western Window* during the 1995 New York Open Center conference in the Czech Republic. *Left to right*: Thomas Hakl, Jay Kinney, and Nicholas Goodrick-Clarke.

PHOTOGRAPH BY THE AUTHOR

who had grown up in England and then moved back to the Czech Republic. Vladislav and I developed a fruitful partnership. He published my Rosicrucian book and later my novel *Return of the Tetrad* in Czech, and I wrote a number of articles for his esoteric magazine *Logos*. I also developed a lasting friendship with Michal Pober, who later moved to the charming town of Kutna Hora, where he was instrumental in setting up a museum of alchemy. Sadly, Michal has since died, and the museum is no longer in existence.

A month later came another significant trip—this time to the Frankfurt Book Fair, which I attended partly on behalf of my institute and partly wearing my author's hat. It was a fruitful visit in several ways. I clinched a deal with Donald Weiser to publish a new edition of the Rosicrucian book, and I interested the British publisher I. B. Tauris in considering a new edition of the book on Ludwig II, which in due course appeared. But there was an even more significant meeting—another of those chance meetings that have so deeply affected the course of my life. One day I was walking through one of the vast, crowded exhibition halls of the Book Fair when I saw a face I knew. It was Frederic Lamond, a familiar figure in the London occult scene, who had been in the witchcraft revival movement known as Wicca since its very early days and had known and worked with Gerald Gardner, the man who had almost single-handedly created the neo-witchcraft religion in Britain. Fred had written a book about his path to Wicca, entitled *Religion without Beliefs*, and was looking for a publisher. We exchanged contact details, and a few weeks later he came to Hamburg with his young German wife, Hildegard, and we had a pleasant dinner together at their hotel. Fred, although he had grown up in England, was partly of Austrian extraction and had recently moved back there and bought his father's house in Carinthia.

Fast-forward to August 1997 and another Open Center conference, this time in Prague to coincide with a series of exhibitions in various locations around the city about the emperor Rudolf II and his court. Among my friends at the conference was Fred Lamond, who came bearing freshly printed copies of his book *Religion without Beliefs*,[2] which he had published at his own expense. I bought a copy from him, read it on the train going home, and was deeply impressed. The book was divided into three parts. The first addressed what Fred called the spiritual bankruptcy of the modern Western world, the second was an account of his own path to paganism as well as his reflections on paganism as a whole, and the third was a description of paganism as practiced in his own tradition of Wicca. Paganism, as he presented it, was a life-affirming, nature-affirming, joyful religion, based not on the blind acceptance of belief but on knowledge and experience of the divine as manifested in the world—hence the title *Religion without Beliefs*. Instead of the patriarchal God of the monotheists there were various forms of polytheism, some involving just a goddess and a god, as in Wicca, others encompassing a multiplicity of deities.

Fig. 8.4. Frederic Lamond in the early 1970s. Fred was a devoted member of the Wicca movement for most of his life and an eloquent apologist for paganism.
PHOTOGRAPH BY THE LATE JEAN MORTON-WILLIAMS, IN THE COLLECTION OF RUTH BAYER

Particularly moving was Fred's description of the life-changing event that had brought him to Wicca. While a student at Bruges in Belgium in the 1950s he fell in love with a Belgian girl called Mary and became engaged to her. For some time the relationship was chaste, but then, at her initiative, they slept together. Here is how he described the experience:

> As she climaxed, I was suddenly catapulted out of space and time into cosmic consciousness. I was all the males of all ages and species making love to all the females of all time, while around us all the other couples were watching us like bodhisattvas in a Tibetan mandala, nodding approvingly as if to say: "Well done! Welcome to the club!"
>
> In my head, a gentle but strong female voice was saying: "All the empires and political systems, all the dogmas, philosophies and ideologies that men have formulated since the dawn of history, put together weigh less in the divine scales than a single embrace of two young lovers, or a single smile on the lips of a new-born infant as it gazes on its mother for the first time."[3]

Sadly he and Mary did not marry, as she realized that marrying into her very conservative Catholic family would hinder Fred in his spiritual development. He, being convinced that he had experienced the presence of the great universal Goddess, set about searching for others who worshipped her. Having read Gerald Gardner's book *Witchcraft Today*, he contacted the author and was soon initiated into Gardner's coven in a cottage at Bricket Wood, Hertfordshire. To quote *Religion without Beliefs* again:

> When the blindfold was removed from my eyes, and I found myself in a dark incense-filled candlelit cottage surrounded by naked figures, I felt again the presence of the same divine power

whom I first encountered in Mary's arms. And when the acting
High Priestess read *The Charge of the Goddess*, I felt this power
welcoming me home![4]

By the time I finished the book I had decided to embrace paganism. I was fifty-four years old—an age when many people are already
set in their ways and attitudes. But here I was about to enter a whole
new world that would bring new vistas, new friends, new opportunities, new meaning and . . . I was about to say "new gods," but I should
rather say "old gods rediscovered."

9

The Gods on
Forty-Second Street

The title of this chapter comes from a remarkable lecture by the late James Hillman,[1] a psychologist and the founder of archetypal psychology, who quotes the mythologist Joseph Campbell as saying: "The gods are right on the corner of Broadway and Forty-Second Street, waiting for the lights to change." Hillman goes on to pose the question whether the gods have truly fled. Indeed, can they leave the world at all? "If they *are* the world," Hillman asks, "how can they be separated from it? Are they not the immortality of the world, giving every item of this world its inherent transcendence, its sublime enchantment, imagination and beauty?" Hillman argues eloquently that polytheism is superior to monotheism as a way of understanding the human mind. In his essay "Many Gods, Many Persons," he writes: "We would consider Artemis, Persephone, Athena, Aphrodite, for instance, as more adequate psychological backgrounds to the complexity of human nature than the unified image of Maria, and the diversity expressed by Apollo, Hermes, Dionysus and Hercules, for instance, to correspond better with psychological actualities than any single idea of self, or single figure of Eros, or of Jesus and Yahweh."[2]

In his book *Revisioning Psychology* Hillman recommends treating the gods as real and working with them.[3] For example, he says that when we have love problems we should put ourselves in touch with Aphrodite, the goddess of love, and try to find out what she has in mind for us. He also has a fascinating concept of the soul. In his view the soul is not an individual thing that each of us possesses, but rather a kind of field of consciousness in which we are all immersed. For Hillman we all have various inner daimons, which are like patterns in the soul-field and toward which we have a responsibility in the eyes of the gods to exercise stewardship.

Not surprisingly, Hillman is at odds with the mainstream of modern psychology. He writes: "Psychology does not even use the word soul: a person is referred to as a self or an ego. Both the world out there and in here have gone through the same process of de-personification. We have all been de-souled. . . . What is needed is a re-visioning, a fundamental shift of perspective out of that soulless predicament we call modern consciousness."[4]

Hillman was for a time a pupil and disciple of the great Swiss psychologist Carl Gustav Jung, whom some would see as also a kind of Pagan on account of his concept of the archetypes, inherited motifs or figures that are present in what Jung called the collective unconscious of humanity. These include the Shadow, the Animus, the Anima, the Wise Old Woman, the Wise Old Man, the Trickster, and the Hero, among others. This notion I find persuasive. I can see, for example, how the gray-bearded Creator God, depicted in Renaissance art, would correspond to the archetype of the Wise Old Man. And in the secular realm the image of the elderly Karl Marx, with his aureole of white hair and beard, would suggest the same archetype. Jung saw the gods as personifications of the archetypes, and in an essay written in 1936 he spoke of Wotan (Odin) as an archetype that had returned in full force in the form of the Nazi movement—a warning that if you try to banish the gods they will return in a disguised and often more dangerous form.

It is no wonder that the gods are irate. Centuries of missionizing zeal and forced conversion have despoiled their sacred places, while they, themselves, have been banished, appropriated as Christian saints, or confined to museums where they lie, neatly labeled and isolated from their true environments. On visits to the Louvre Museum in Paris I used to admire the statue called the Winged Victory of Samothrace, not knowing that the island of Samothrace in the Aegean was one of the holiest places of the ancient world, a center of initiation into the mysteries and the site of a great temple complex, where all that remains today, after Muslim and Christian depredation, are a few columns, a circular arena, and a few other relics lying forlorn amid overgrown remains of foundations. The Winged Victory, itself, was carried off in the nineteenth century by the French diplomat and amateur archaeologist Charles Champoiseau.[5] Many similar sacrileges were perpetrated wherever the missionizing zealots went. In 724 CE the English missionary Boniface cut down an oak tree sacred to Thor/Donar at the town of Geismar in what is now the German state of Hessen. And some half a century later the Irminsul, the sacred pillar of Saxons, was cut down on the orders of the Frankish king Charlemagne, who also forbade the worship of springs or trees. Those who broke this law were fined, and those who refused baptism were condemned to death.

Yet, despite all efforts to eliminate them, the old gods have managed to survive. In my story "Master of the Starlit Grove," in the collection of the same name, I introduce the idea of a pagan egregore, that is to say a thoughtform on the etheric plane, created by many people thinking the same thoughts, working with the same symbols, and focusing on some powerful central idea. The story puts forward the idea that, at the time of the forced Christianization of Europe, a group of Pagans came together and created an egregore as a sort of ark to preserve paganism until the influence of Christianity diminished and the old gods could reemerge.[6]

This of course is fiction, but I believe there is something like a pagan egregore, which has helped the gods to live on over the centuries. Over much of the world the worship of the old ones has continued up to the present day. Even in Europe there are Indigenous peoples, such as the Mari in Russia and some communities of the Sámi in northern Scandinavia, who remain loyal to their ancient pagan ways. And in other regions—in Africa, Asia, Australia, and North and South America—there are many Indigenous peoples practicing their traditional religions as they have always done, despite the missionizing efforts of the colonial powers. This is particularly noticeable in countries that resisted colonization, such as Japan and Korea.

Growing up in Britain, I think I first became aware of the old gods when I learned how four days of the week are named after them: Tuesday after Tyr, the god of courage and self-sacrifice; Wednesday after Woden, Odin, or Wotan; Thursday after Thor, the thunder god; and Friday after Freya, the goddess of love. Later I learned how they live on in certain geographical names. One of Odin's alternative names is Grim, meaning the "masked one," which appears in place names like Grimsby. The very name of Britain comes from the Romano-Celtic goddess Brigantia (meaning something like the "High One"), who in Ireland became transformed into Saint Brigid.

A god who appears to have exerted a particular fascination in Britain is Pan, the goat-legged, flute-playing god of nature, of shepherds, and of wild abandon. In the 1870s he appeared in the painting *Pan and Psyche* by Sir Edward Burne-Jones, and in 1894 in a drawing by Aubrey Beardsley on the title page of Arthur Machen's story *The Great God Pan*. Aleister Crowley's poem "Hymn to Pan" followed

Fig. 9.1. *Pan and Psyche*: a painting by Edward Burne-Jones, 1872.
See also color plate 4.

in 1897. And in 1906 his English equivalent, Puck, appeared in
Rudyard Kipling's book *Puck of Pook's Hill*. Evidently, under the surface in Britain, land of hope and glory, of solid respectability and
of shopkeepers, there was a yearning for something wild, free, and
pagan, something that the British mind saw embodied in the figure
of Pan. He featured again in the 1936 novel *The Goat-Foot God* by
the occultist Dion Fortune (real name Violet Firth, 1890–1947),

which made a deep impression on me when I read it in my late twenties. The epigraph at the beginning is a stirring poem to Pan, the first two verses of which read as follows:

> *Came the voice of Destiny,*
> *Calling o'er the Ionian Sea,*
> *"The Great God Pan is dead, is dead.*
> *Humbled is the horned head;*
> *Shut the door that hath no key—*
> *Waste the vales of Arcady."*
> *Shackled by the Iron Age,*
> *Lost the woodland heritage,*
> *Heavy goes the heart of man,*
> *Parted from the light-foot Pan;*
> *Wearily he wears a chain*
> *Till the Goat-god comes again.*[7]

This poem is a part of a ritual called the Rite of Pan, written by Dion Fortune for her magical order, the Fraternity of the Inner Light (now the Society of the Inner Light). She argued that the modern world needed the lustful, visceral, exuberant force of Pan, which she called "vitamin P." She felt that something valuable was lost to humanity when the ancient gods were suppressed with the onslaught of Christianity. In *The Goat-Foot God* she reflects on the revival of the gods during the Renaissance: "It is a curious fact that when men began to re-assemble the fragments of Greek culture—the peerless statues of the gods and the ageless wisdom of the sages—a Renaissance came to the civilization that had sat in intellectual darkness since the days when the gods had withdrawn before the assaults of the Galileans."[8] Dion Fortune writes about the gods from the perspective of a trained psychotherapist. The hero of *The Goat-Foot God* is Hugh Paston who, at the beginning of the story, is a disoriented young man, lacking purpose and drive. By working magically with the Pan principle he gains a new vigor and forcefulness, enabling him to win the woman he loves.

Pan also features in another of my favorite novels, *The Blessing of Pan*, by the Anglo-Irish writer Lord Dunsany (1878–1957), originally published in 1928. This is the story of how an English village is gradually taken over by the spirit of Pan. It starts off with the local vicar hearing, in the twilight, the sound of a flute wafting out over the village and playing an eerie, hypnotic melody, causing the villagers to behave in odd ways. He sees them going off into the woods at night and hears reports of weird rituals being performed there. Worried about these developments, he writes to the bishop, who merely tells him that he should take a week's holiday at Brighton, where a bit of sea air will do him good. And another priest that he speaks to about the problem advises him to get the young lads of the village to play more cricket so as to take their minds off any silliness they might be tempted to get up to. So the vicar is left alone to deal with the situation as best he can. He starts to investigate what is going on and slowly finds himself coming under the spell of Pan until finally he succumbs to it completely.

Pan is a protean god, and in Gerald Gardner's Wicca movement he became the Horned God, consort to the Great Goddess who, as Gardner writes, quoting the invocation called the Charge of the Goddess, "was also called among men Artemis, Astarte, Dione, Melusine, Aphrodite and many other names."[9] This was she who, back in the 1950s, revealed herself to my friend Frederic Lamond in the ecstasy of love-making, as I described earlier, causing him to go on a search for others who revered the Goddess, a search that led him to Wicca as "the only game in town," as he put it to me.

It was to be many years before the Goddess movement became the mass phenomenon that it is today, but Gardner's Wicca was a small plant that was destined to multiply. Another person who celebrated the Goddess in the mid-twentieth century was the poet Robert Graves in his book *The White Goddess* (1948). I remember reading the book around the late 1960s and being struck by the final chapter headed "Return of the Goddess," in which he says the following: "Only after a period of complete political and religious disorganization can the suppressed desire of the Western races, which is for some form of Goddess-worship, with her love not limited to maternal benevolence and her afterworld not deprived of a sea, find satisfaction at last."[10] This I could agree with, although I was not yet ready to accept the full implications, which would inevitably have involved embracing some form of paganism.

Today, anyone on a similar search to the one that Fred Lamond undertook would only have to go to the internet and they would find not only Goddess-worshipping groups in abundance but thousands of other groups in many different countries following various pagan paths, ranging from Asatru to the revived paganism of ancient Greece. They would be able to watch a film about Thor or Beowulf, attend a concert by one of the numerous pop groups in the pagan scene, or listen to a lecture or read a book on some aspect of paganism.

If such a searcher were to delve into scholarly and scientific literature, they would soon discover that among psychologists and philosophers there is a small but vociferous and growing polytheistic faction. I have mentioned the psychologist James Hillman as an example. Hillman was one of most frequent speakers at the Eranos conferences, a series of meetings held at Ascona, Switzerland, from 1933 to explore the inner and spiritual traditions of the world and the interface between East and West in an interdisciplinary spirit. Thomas Hakl, in his monumental book on the project, *Eranos: An Alternative Intellectual History of the Twentieth Century* (translated from German by myself and Hereward Tilton), describes a debate that took place there between the monotheistic and polytheistic factions among the speakers.[11] Hillman was one of the latter. Another was the scholar of religion and literature David Miller, author of *The New Polytheism: Rebirth of the Gods and Goddesses.*[12]

One of the most eloquent apologies for paganism has been made by the French philosopher Alain de Benoist in his book *On Being a Pagan* (*Comment peut-on être païen?*), first published in 1981. De Benoist shares Nietzsche's view that "the conversion of Europe to Christianity . . . was one of the most catastrophic events in world history."[13] At the same time he perceives a pagan undercurrent in Europe that has remained alive and has come to the surface from time to time. Paganism for de Benoist means upholding mythos over logos, or in other words, magic and mystery over the reign of rationality and the literal word, and the notion of an eternal return over that of a creation of the world *ex nihilo*. He urges us to become familiar with our ancient Indo-European religious heritage. Altogether he makes a good philosophical case for paganism, but gives rather short shrift to pagan practice. "Contemporary paganism," he says "does not consist in erecting altars to Apollo or reviving the worship of Odin."[14] But why not? That is precisely what many modern Pagans are doing. In fact I have a stele to Apollo in our garden among other works invoking the old gods. What good is philosophizing about the gods unless one actively celebrates them?

Traditionally there is a gulf between the world of the anthropologists, philosophers, and scholars of religion on the one hand, and the world of active Pagans on the other, but now I observe a certain amount of overlap between the two. An interesting example was the role played by the American author Michael Harner (1929–2018) in reviving shamanism among the Sámi population in Norway. In the seventeenth and eighteenth centuries shamanism had been virtually extinguished in Norway through an aggressive conversion campaign by Lutheran zealots, but in the 1980s Ailo Gaup, a young Norwegian of Sámi descent, created a revival after being trained in shamanic techniques by Harner in California. Some people have criticized this revived shamanism as inauthentic, but a reinvented shamanism is surely better than none, and to me this case is an example of how valuable the synergy between the academic and the practitioner can be.

10

The Fivefold Path

Reflecting on the steps that had led me toward paganism, I realized that I had been searching for a spiritual path that would be satisfying on various levels, and initially I conceived of four levels: soul, mind, heart, and belly. Mainstream Christianity has much for the soul and heart, a certain amount for the mind, but virtually nothing for the belly, that is to say the visceral, Dionysiac part of our being. Wicca offers much for the soul, heart, and belly, but not so much for the mind. Judaism has something for all four levels, but still I felt it was ultimately not for me. Thinking about this recently, I realized that, in addition to soul, mind, heart, and belly, we have a fifth important component, namely the feet. I hear the reader exclaim: "Did you say 'feet'?!" Yes, the feet—or rather the ground on which they stand, that is to say the land with which we feel a connection, whether by birth or because we have chosen to put down roots there. And by the land I mean everything that goes with it—the geography, the nature, the wildlife, the spirits of place, the inhabitants and their traditions, customs, crafts, languages, music, dances, and of course their religious beliefs and practices and sacred places. For me, all of these things are part of an organic whole. I have already described how, looking back across the Atlantic from New York, I realized that I was a north European. So, when I moved back to Europe and turned to the pagan path, I wanted to celebrate the ancient pagan gods of the region, as my ancestors had done, and I wanted a ceremonial practice that brought a sense of continuity with the past.

Gardnerian Wicca might have been an option, but it had only two deities, the God and the Goddess, whereas I wanted to celebrate a multiplicity of gods. Moreover, Wicca was not rooted in a particular region, and it was essentially an invention of the twentieth century, a bricolage put together by Gardner from elements of Freemasonry, Golden Dawn magic, mythology, European folklore, and the writings of the American ethnologist Charles Godfrey Leland. So I was not yet at the end of my pagan journey, although I was immensely grateful to Fred Lamond for helping to bring me this far.

After returning to Hamburg from Prague I telephoned Fred and asked him what I should do next, and he suggested that I join the Pagan Federation, an organization that had started in England but had become international, which I did fairly quickly through a couple who were the coordinators for its German branch. They in turn suggested that I start what in England is called a "pub moot" and in Germany a *"Stammtisch"*—a regular gathering of like-minded souls in some convivial hostelry. They gave me the name and telephone number of Oliver, who had run such a pub moot in Bremen, and Oliver gave me the names of some Hamburg Pagans. However, it took me some time to get round to actually organizing the moot, and it was February of 1999 before the first meeting took place. As the venue I chose a cozy bistro called Variable in a slightly Bohemian district of Hamburg called the Karolinenviertel. There was heavy snow that evening, and I was afraid no one would come, but in the event nine people turned up, including Susanne, a homoeopath; Angelika, an ethnologist writing a master's dissertation on neo-paganism; "Arkana" (real name Henning), a "priest of the old religion" whose day job I forget; Andreas, who ran a mail-order business selling oils and incenses; Angela and Karin, who ran a female witches' group; and another Andreas, a graphic designer.

Over the three years or so that the moot existed, people dropped out and others joined. In terms of religious direction it was eclectic. Some of the members professed a vaguely Celtic type of paganism, some called themselves Wiccans, some followed the Nordic path. We began to carry out rituals together to celebrate the seasonal festivals, sometimes in a member's flat, sometimes in a local park, mixing traditions to keep everybody happy. We would follow a fairly standard procedure for such rituals, casting a circle by invoking the powers of the quarters and the elements, calling to this or that deity, sharing reflections on the occasion, and passing a horn of mead or some other beverage.

Soon I felt these eclectic rituals to be rather bland and lacking in vital energy, and I began to associate and celebrate more and more with the Nordic faction within the group. There were many reasons why I was attracted to the Nordic tradition or Asatru, to use the widely accepted name, which means faithfulness to the Aesir, one of the two groups of Nordic gods (the other is the Vanir). I found that Asatru had force, fire, passion, and a certain wild, free energy, like an untamed horse—strong, beautiful, proud, and somehow noble. I have described earlier how, during my New York period, my then-girlfriend Deborah got me to practice a breathing technique involving hyperventilation that was designed to remove physical and emotional blockages, and how during two sessions I experienced the release of a powerful sub-personality that came forth with a deafening roar like something between a caveman and a gorilla. In the Asatru rituals I have the feeling that this part of me is welcomed and accepted and can express itself in a sovereign way. Moreover, unlike the Gardnerian Wicca movement, Asatru has a certain continuity from pre-Christian times. Admittedly it is to a great extent a reconstruction, but still there is much that has survived from those earlier times: the collection of old Norse poems called the *Edda* with its wealth of mythological lore, the Icelandic sagas, the numerous archaeological remains such as megaliths and ship burials, the folk customs, the oral traditions, and of course the runic alphabet, which is not just an alphabet but a set of powerfully charged symbols.

Above all, I felt that Asatru was the religion of my roots. I have already spoken of my family genealogy. I am partly Celtic through the McIntosh line and partly Germanic through my mother's Anglo-Saxon heritage. On my mother's side I also believe there was some Scandinavian influx into my genes through the ancestor called Sigmundr whom I mentioned earlier. Perhaps there are particular ancestors who speak to us out of the past. At any rate, it seemed to me that Sigmundr and my Nordic forebears were calling me to the Nordic path.

I am aware that some people have a prejudice against Asatru and similar movements working with the Nordic tradition, linking them with fascist and white supremacist tendencies. What I usually reply, when I hear somebody make this accusation, is: If you were a peace-loving Muslim, would you give up your religion because of the extremists who commit violent acts in its name? While there are a few extremist elements in some of the groups following the Nordic way—as there are in most religions—they are a small minority and not typical of the religion as a whole.

While I pursued the pagan path I was kept very busy in my working life: editing my journal and supervising the publications program, attending conferences for the Institute, some in faraway places like Australia and Botswana, preparing reports for our annual board meeting, and acting as public relations officer. In what little spare time I had I worked on the book on sacred and symbolic gardens that was eventually published as *Gardens of the Gods*, but I found it difficult to clear the necessary mental space. In 1998 I took an unpaid sabbatical of about four months, partly in order to get on with the book. For about three quarters of that time I was based in my flat in north London.

I was able to make some progress with the writing, but it was to be another seven years before *Gardens of the Gods* was actually published.

Among the highlights of my life during the late 1990s and early 2000s was a series of meetings of a group called the Palladian Academy. The initiative came from Joscelyn Godwin, who had the idea of organizing an informal private seminar for a group of like-minded friends sharing a scholarly interest in esoteric matters. As a venue he found the Villa Saraceno, a magnificent Palladian mansion near Venice, which belonged to the British conservation organization, the Landmark Trust, and there we met in January 1997. There were ten of us altogether, including some prominent names in the area of esoteric studies, such as Professor Antoine Faivre of the Sorbonne, and some who were to go on to distinguished careers in the field, such as Wouter Hanegraaff and Marco Pasi. At each session there was a talk from one of the participants, followed by a discussion.

We all found it so enjoyable that we decided to hold further meetings, and two years later a second meeting was organized in Styria, Austria, by my friend Hans Thomas Hakl, businessman, scholar, and possessor of one of the largest collections of esoteric books in the world. At that meeting we were joined by Nicholas Goodrick-Clarke and his wife, Clare. From 2001 onward the meetings were held at a medieval château in the south of France, the Domaine de Taurenne, belonging to Rosalie Basten, a Dutch businesswoman with a profound interest in esoteric matters, who was the founder and financial backer of the Chair for Hermetic Philosophy and Related Currents at the University of Amsterdam, an initiative that sprang partly from the seed planted by the Palladian Academy. Some half-dozen meetings took place at the Domaine de Taurenne at intervals of about two years. These were unforgettable events. The talks and discussions often took place in the courtyard of the château with the gentle splashing of a fountain as background music. And there were long, convivial, open-air dinners on a terrace overlooking a swimming

Fig. 10.1. A meeting of the Palladian Academy,
Château de Taurenne, circa 2002. *Left to right*: Antoine Faivre,
Arthur Versluis, Thomas Hakl, Wouter Hanegraaff.

PHOTOGRAPH BY THE AUTHOR

pool. One of the initiatives that came out of these meetings was the creation, also with the participation and backing of Rosalie Basten, of a learned society, the European Society for the Study of Western Esotericism (ESSWE), which is now well established with its own journal, *Aries*, and a series of conferences. With the creation of the ESSWE conferences, much of the raison d'être of the Taurenne meetings was removed, so eventually they ceased.

The academic study of esotericism took a further step forward with the foundation of a new chair at the University of Exeter in England. This was thanks to Nicholas Goodrick-Clarke, who approached the university and persuaded them to found a unit within the history department called the Exeter Centre for the Study of Esotericism, offering a distance MA course. He, himself, was appointed to the chair, and he proceeded to assemble a staff of part-time lecturers including myself. The Centre opened its doors in the autumn of 2005 and quickly attracted highly motivated students of many age groups and professions, who came not only from Britain but from as far and wide as Alaska, Canada, Sweden, Denmark, and Romania. There were two or three seminars in Exeter each year, and in between the students were given reading lists and essays to write and could consult with the faculty by email or telephone. The Centre was unique in the world in offering a distance MA in the study of esotericism, and as such was greatly cherished by the students. So it was a great blow when in 2012 Nicholas Goodrick-Clarke died very suddenly and unexpectedly. The program continued for a year under Clare's direction and then folded. Subsequently the university established a similar initiative, the Centre for Magic and Esotericism, which offers an MA in magic and occult sciences.

Meanwhile I continued to take part periodically in the New York Open Center conferences. One that stands out in my mind was held in Florence in 2000. We met in a beautiful Renaissance palace close to the city center, where we could take coffee breaks in a bougainvillea-scented garden. One evening we spent in another palace high on a hill overlooking the city where we were treated to a performance of Renaissance music and dance with the performers in period costumes. The final dinner of the conference was in a restaurant where the landlord, himself an esotericist, had made in our honor a special door with alchemical symbols, at the entrance to our private dining room. After the conference I teamed up with Ruth, one of the participants, for a post-conference excursion. We didn't start a love affair but had a delightful trip, visiting Assisi and the Tarot Garden of Niki de Saint-Phalle at Capalbio.

By now the world had moved into the twenty-first century and the third millennium, although strictly speaking the second millennium lasted until the end of 2000. Never mind. What everyone called the new millennium started with mass parties, firework displays, and extravagant public happenings. In London they built the Millennium Dome where a great spectacle took place, celebrating British achievements such as the National Health Service. But, from the perspective of the time in which I am writing, with the National Health Service falling apart, cities decaying, poverty rife, politics in disarray, and a general mood of despondency in the air of Britain, the millennial celebrations now seem like a hollow promise.

In Germany there was Expo 2000 in Hannover, which I attended along with colleagues to represent the UNESCO Institute. Its title was *"Mensch, Natur und Technik—Eine neue Welt entsteht"* (Humans, Nature and Technology—A New World Emerges). All kinds of technological wonders were displayed including a gigantic mechanical hand that reached down, picked up a Volkswagen beetle like some giant's toy, held it in the air, and then put it down again. I was left thinking: This is all very well, but what is it all for? Unless it serves a deeper human purpose it is merely an empty display. It was a great relief when I flew directly from Hannover to the above-mentioned Open Center conference in Florence to spend several days being uplifted by real beauty and wisdom amid incomparable surroundings.

My journey along the pagan path continued. By then I had found a convivial group of friends in the Nordic pagan or Asatru tradition with whom I celebrated the seasonal festivals and attended a pub moot in the harbor area of Hamburg. Some of us, who wanted to dig deeper, formed a group for the study of Nordic mythology, which met at my flat. There would be a talk followed by a discussion. One of the participants at these meetings was Jörg Rohfeld, who became a deeply valued friend and a close companion on my spiritual path. He had been one of the leading activists in the Nordic revival in Germany and had a profound knowledge of the Nordic religion, mythology, and traditions. The deeper I went into the study of that domain, the more I realized what a richly fascinating and beautiful world I had discovered.

In the summer of 2003 I went to Iceland to visit Hilmar and to attend his installation as the newly elected Allsherjargoði (High Priest) of the Asatru community there. It was an unforgettable visit. The installation itself took place at the Thingvellir, the site of the ancient Icelandic parliament, located at a point where a rift in the Earth's crust forms a passage between two walls of rock. Hilmar and a group of Asatru priests and priestesses, dressed in ceremonial costumes, mounted a rocky promontory, watched by a crowd assembled on a grassy bank below, where many colorful banners were in evidence. Torches and a fire bowl flared in the pearly midsummer evening light. Passages were read aloud from the *Edda* and the ancient Icelandic legal code. Hilmar was sworn in as Allsherjargoði, drank from a mead horn,

Fig. 10.2. Installation of Hilmar Örn Hilmarsson as head of the
Asatru community in Iceland, 2003.

PHOTOGRAPH BY THE AUTHOR

Fig. 10.3. Hilmar Örn Hilmarsson conducting a kind of
Asatru baptism ceremony for Julius Samúelsson.
The boy is Julius's son Thorvaldur. In the background,
left to right: Ólafur Sigurdsson, Lara Jóna Thorsteinsdóttir,
Janna Kristín Berg. See also color plate 5.

PHOTOGRAPH BY THE AUTHOR

and then delivered his inaugural speech. I also witnessed a kind of
Asatru baptism ceremony for a young man, who stood with his small
son while Hilmar pronounced some words of blessing.

Afterward I spent a few more days traveling in Iceland with
Hilmar as my guide. Although Iceland has been officially Christian
since the year 1000, it's a country where the old pagan roots are
still strong, where the *Edda* is a national treasure, where streets are
named after gods, and where belief in the elves is widespread. A couple living in a remote area told us that they had received a visit from

two building inspectors in connection with a plan to build an out-house, and the first question the inspectors had asked was whether there were elves on the site. As the answer was no, the inspectors were happy and the outhouse was duly built. In other cases building plans have been altered and roads diverted so as not to infringe on elf territory.

By that time there had been major changes in my life. That same year, 2003, I left the UNESCO Institute and moved to a house that I had bought in the village of Rühstädt in Brandenburg, which I had already been using as a weekend retreat for some time. The house was a charming half-timbered building attached to a disused flour mill. The village, located in the middle of a large nature reserve, was famous on account of the many storks who nested on the rooftops from early spring to around August. The surrounding countryside reminded me of the England of *Wind in the Willows*—sleepy mead-ows with cows grazing, deep woodlands, meandering rivers, long avenues of majestic oak trees. It was an idyll. I planned to settle there for the rest of my life, but the Norns of fate had other plans for me, as very soon became clear.

11

Witchcraft in Hamburg

The crucial new turn of events happened through the Museum of Ethnology in Hamburg, located in the Rothenbaumchaussee, almost next door to the UNESCO Institute. The museum possesses a unique collection of books and artifacts relating to witchcraft (the *Hexenarchiv*), which was assembled in the twentieth century by a folk high school teacher called Johann Kruse with the intention of exposing the notion of witchcraft as a benighted superstition. Over the years this collection has attracted a good deal of attention both from scholars and, ironically, from modern-day witches and occultists. Realizing the importance of the collection, the museum in 2001 mounted a big exhibition on the history of witchcraft and in parallel offered a series of related lectures and rituals. I gave a lecture on the revival of paganism, and I attended two rituals led by Dr. Donate Pahnke of the University of Bremen, who had a reputation as a respected scholar of religion.

Later I learned just how impressive her background was. Not content with training and practicing as a physiotherapist, then marrying and having two daughters, she had studied as a mature student at the University of Bremen, then gone on to take a PhD in religious studies and to embark on a distinguished career as a scholar and university lecturer. Her specialties were gender studies, neo-paganism, and in particular the neo-witchcraft movement—indeed she was the first person in Germany to write about present-day witches in a scholarly way. She was much in demand as a lecturer, both in Bremen and elsewhere, and she had a string of publications to her credit, including her pioneering doctoral thesis "*Ethik und Geschlecht*" (Ethics and Gender, 1991). What made her even more remarkable was that she was also a ritual practitioner and a priestess in the neo-pagan Reclaiming Community, which had been founded in the United States by Starhawk (alias Miriam Simos) and had then spread to many other countries.

From her reputation I sensed her to be a kindred spirit, as I also wore two hats—as a scholar and a practitioner—and I was curious to meet her. Attending her rituals in the museum I found her to be a woman of striking radiance and charisma, but I was one of about a hundred participants and a conversation with her was impossible. However, another opportunity came two years later when the museum held a symposium dealing with the treatment of the theme of witchcraft in museums. I was invited to give a talk on the pagan revival, and I was scheduled to speak immediately after Donate, who was due to lecture about the modern witchcraft movement and the rituals in the museum. We conferred by telephone beforehand so as to avoid duplication, and duly delivered our talks. On the second day of the conference we got into conversation during a coffee break and—to cut a long story short—we have been inseparable ever since. I was the sailor who had found his "harbor of love."

Within three months we had decided to move together. Rühstädt proved to be out of the question, as work opportunities there for Donate were virtually nil. So the following spring we moved into a rented house in Bremen. Donate remembers my entering the house, dropping into a sofa, and saying: "Now at last I have found my home harbor!" We rented out and eventually sold the Rühstädt house. Financially we were on rather thin ice. Donate taught courses at the university, spoke at conferences, and also had a practice as a spiritual counselor. I kept busy writing, editing, translating, and doing some English teaching at the University of Bremen.

In 2006 we became engaged in Weimar, where we were scouting out accommodation for a forthcoming Esoteric Quest of the New York Open Center. It was a very cold winter night and we had a candlelight dinner in a cozy corner at the White Swan, Goethe's favorite inn and right beside his beautiful house in the town center, now a museum. What could be a more romantic place to decide to get married? We walked back to our hotel on a cloud of happiness under a clear, starry sky. The Esoteric Quest happened a few months later, starting at Kutna Hora in the Czech Republic and proceeding, via the famous spa of Marienbad, to Weimar in Germany. I gave two talks, and Donate led three rituals for the participants.

In the same year I was called back to the UNESCO Institute for two years to fill a gap left by the sudden departure of my successor. In the autumn of the same year we were married at full moon after the magical interval of three years and three days since our first meeting. We wanted both a regular registry office wedding and a pagan handfasting, so for the venue we chose the Lür-Kropp-Hof, a former farm property on beautiful grounds that had a facility for the official proceedings as well as a wonderful converted barn for the handfasting.

We wanted a handfasting that we would both be happy with, so we agreed on a mixture of Asatru and Donate's form of pagan spirituality, involving a strong emphasis on the Goddess and influenced by the Reclaiming tradition in which she had been active for many years, teaching, priestessing, and organizing. Hilmar came over from Iceland to conduct the ceremony together with a friend of Donate. We sat down together on the day before the wedding to plan the proceedings and came up with a ritual that combined elements of both our traditions.

On the day of the wedding the gods brought us mild, sunny autumn weather. Family and friends gathered in the Hochtiedshus (Wedding House), a lovely half-timbered outbuilding of the Lür-Kropp-Hof, for the registry office wedding, conducted by a registrar with a wonderful human touch. As we processed into the building my son Jason played the wedding march from Wagner's *Lohengrin* on the piano. Afterward everyone went off for a break and came back in the afternoon for the handfasting, which was a deeply moving ceremony, beginning with Jörg Rohfeld blowing a horn at the start, and culminating in Hilmar holding out an oath ring for us to grasp and take our vows on, according to ancient Norse tradition. Afterward there was a

Fig, 11.1 Jörg Rohfeld blows a horn to announce the beginning of our handfasting in November 2006.

Fig. 11.2. Hilmar holds out the oath ring for us to
grasp and pledge our troth.

PHOTOGRAPH FROM THE COLLECTION OF CHRISTOPHER AND DONATE McINTOSH

dinner with speeches and then much dancing including Scottish reels
and a spiral dance according to the Reclaiming tradition.

The handfasting was a special moment in a life together marked
by a continuous round of seasonal festivals and other pagan celebrations. As I put it in a poem that I wrote for Donate:

> *The windmill of the year turns*
> *And we mark each turn*
> *Side by side in shared ceremony*
> *Warmed by mead and festive blaze.*
> *Under winged stars our Spiral Dance*
> *Of life and love goes on.*

In the same year as our wedding, 2006, my elder son, Angus, and his wife, Susan, and their two children, Daniel and Abigail, moved to Bremen. Angus worked for the firm of Mars, and he had been assigned to one of their subsidiaries, located in the town of Verden, about an hour's drive away. They bought a house in the suburb of Borgfeld, only a couple of miles from ours, and they were there for about nine years, during which time there were many happy family gatherings, and I saw Daniel and Abigail grow into lively teenagers and then into mature young adults. Sadly, Angus and Sue later split up, and Angus moved to Hamburg, where he now lives with his wife, Katja. Meanwhile my younger son, Jason, and his wife, Natalia, had had two sons, Leo and John. They lived in London, but later moved to Tring in Hertfordshire, close to Berkhamsted where I had spent so many years during my first marriage.

In Donate I now had a soulmate who was on the same spiritual wavelength as myself. Our respective pagan paths were slightly different, but complemented each other well. Donate led a seasonal ritual group called Mondgarten (Moon Garden), which I became part of. It celebrated the equinoxes and solstices as well as the four Celtic festivals of Brigid (or Imbolc), Beltane, Lammas (or Lughnasad), and Samhain (Halloween). Each festival has certain special features. For example, at midsummer we make a wreath of corn sheaves and roses, which we burn in an extra ceremony in the period between Christmas and January 6 to bid farewell to the old year and herald the new one. To begin with we held the rituals in a hired room in a women's center in Bremen, where Donate had offered all eight seasonal festivals every year for about thirty years for women only, then founded Mondgarten for women and men in 2008. After a couple of years we changed over to celebrating at home with a smaller group, as we still do.

I continued on my parallel Asatru path. Living in Bremen, I was now not far from my close friend and fellow Asatruar, Jörg, who had

Fig. 11.3. Donate
drumming in our
garden in Bremen.
See also color plate 6.
PHOTOGRAPH BY THE AUTHOR

Fig. 11.4. Helping to make a wreath of corn and roses during a
midsummer ritual at our home in 2013. See also color plate 7.

PHOTOGRAPH BY DONATE MCINTOSH

bought a secluded piece of land surrounded by meadows in an area lying to the south of the Elbe estuary, which he had begun to transform into a sacred space for celebrating the equinoxes and solstices. I first took part in a ritual there in the summer of 2003, when the place was just an open field. Over time Jörg developed the site with loving care, planting a ring of birch trees with a fire pit in the center encircled by stones, shaping the branches at one side into a sort of open-air altar, making a winding path to the birch grove, and placing a wooden pole halfway along the path to serve as a watcher or guardian of the approach to the sanctuary. He had also made an alternative and more easily accessible ritual site adjacent to his parental home

Fig. 11.5. Jörg Rohfeld working at his ritual site
in the Wingst near Cuxhaven.

PHOTOGRAPH BY THE AUTHOR

in a nearby village, where we could celebrate when the weather was particularly cold or inclement. We called our ritual group *Langhus* (a Low German word meaning "Long House"). In addition, Jörg was active in a countrywide Asatru organization called the Verein für germanisches Heidentum (Association for Germanic Heathenry), which I also later joined. Tragically, Jörg died in 2020 at the age of fifty-six from the delayed aftereffects of a stroke.

The seasonal celebrations have become an important part of my life. Each one offers an opportunity to reflect on what that particular moment in the cycle of the year means to me, but also to think about where I am in the greater cycle of my life and what message the gods, spirits, or ancestors might have for me at that time. In these ceremonies I connect with my roots and reach out, heart to heart, to those celebrating with me in a shared ritual, lovingly performed. When people ask me what is the use of such things I sometimes reply by quoting the words of W. B. Yeats in his poem "A Prayer for My Daughter":

> *How but in custom and in ceremony*
> *Are innocence and beauty born?*

Apart from my involvement in Langhus and the Verein für germanisches Heidentum, I am conscious of being part of an international heathen community. Some highlights of recent years have been my visits to Iceland, where the Asatru community under Hilmar's leadership continues to go from strength to strength and at the time of writing is building an impressive temple on the outskirts of Reykjavik. Other heathen temples have sprung up elsewhere, such as the one at Korinth on the Danish island of Fyn and the Odinist Temple at Newark in England. Then there are the international gatherings of kindred spirits, such as the International Asatru Summer Camp (IASC). The 2012 camp was held conveniently not far from

Fig. 11.6. The author at the 2012 International Asatru
Summer Camp near Bremen.

PHOTOGRAPH FROM THE AUTHOR'S COLLECTION

Bremen at a youth hostel set in beautiful countryside near the village of Sandhatten. It was attended by one hundred or so people from
about twelve different countries, including England, the United States,
France, Poland, Denmark, the Czech Republic, Germany, Spain, and
Norway. There was a similarly international group at the 2015 IASC,
held in the town of Unnaryd in Sweden. On both occasions there was
a rich program of lectures, workshops, and blóts.

As paganism for me has much to do with being connected with a
particular region, I find it important to know the local idiom, which
in this area is Low German (Plattdeutsch), and to cherish and celebrate regional traditions, such as folk songs and folk dancing. These

things tend to be scorned by the modern cultural establishment as being quaint and faintly laughable, when in fact they are often repositories of profound symbolism and traditional wisdom.

Since before I moved to Germany I have been fascinated by Morris dancing, which—although probably originally of Iberian origin—has come to be seen as something quintessentially English. Some of the dances have a pagan or nature-religious character, involving striking the ground with sticks to awaken the forces of nature in the springtime. A Morris team typically consists of six dancers and a fool. The fool often wears an animal mask and a colorful costume such as the so-called Forest of Dean coat, made of tattered strips of cloth. His role is to make fun of the dancers, moving between them, aping their movements, and occasionally striking them with an inflated sheep's bladder or, more likely these days, a balloon. The fool corresponds to the jester, who used to be a familiar feature at many of the courts of Europe. Just as the court jester has to combine wisdom and wit, so the fool has to be the best dancer of all in order to mimic the movements of the others while entertaining the spectators with his antics. There is much wisdom in such ancient folk traditions.

In England I had always loved watching Morris dancers on a summer's day, leaping about on the green in front of some country pub, but only later in life did it occur to me to take it up myself. Inspired by a Morris performance at a pagan conference in Croydon, I discussed with Jörg the possibility of starting a Morris group in Bremen, and he was enthused by the idea. So we got together a group of friends who were willing to take part. Then, through the British organization, the Morris Ring, I contacted Anthony Heywood, an Englishman who lived in Holland and ran a Morris group there. He and his wife, Jennifer, who played the violin, came to Bremen for a weekend and taught us some of the simpler dances.

We called our group the Langhus Folk Dance Group and used to

Fig. 11.7. The Langhus Morris dancing group in the garden of
our house in Bremen. See also color plate 8.

PHOTOGRAPH BY DONATE MCINTOSH

meet about once a fortnight at the English Club near the main station
in Bremen. Soon we expanded our repertoire to include folk dances
of other countries. For a time we were joined by a young Latvian
student called Sandra, who taught us some Latvian dances. We also
did Scottish and north German ones. Live music was sometimes provided by various of our members, such as Werner, who played the
ukulele. On one occasion we held a midsummer dance session in our
garden, much to the delight of our neighbors. Even those who had
not seen the dancing remarked on the beautiful music they had heard
wafting out from behind our house.

I believe that what those neighbors saw or heard satisfied a thirst that they were not consciously aware of until they had taken a draught of what we offered them. I encountered similar reactions from people who witnessed other performances of our group, and this brought home to me how undernourished the public are today by the junk food that passes for most modern music and dance. I underline the word *most*, as there have been certain exciting developments in these areas in modern times. One of the great pioneers of dance was the Hungarian Rudolf Laban (1879–1958), Rosicrucian, esotericist, inventor of a standard form of dance notation, and creator of a dance method intended to develop the faculties of understanding, feeling, and will. The essential idea is that the dancer can connect with the great cosmic dance by moving within the coordinates of the five Platonic solids, especially the dodecahedron (with twelve sides). The dancers start by practicing inside a hollow dodecahedron made of connected rods and then graduate to moving about within an invisible dodecahedron.

The Laban method is part of the syllabus at the Trinity Laban Conservatoire of Music and Dance in southeast London, where in 2008 I attended a conference on Rudolf Laban and took part in a dance workshop. At the workshop the idea was to explore the interface between free and structured movement, and this involved a lot of improvisation. It was very different from the kind of dancing I was used to, but I found it in a way liberating, as I did with the Five Rhythms dance method, which I experienced while visiting the Esalen Institute at Big Sur in California. The method was invented in the 1970s by Gabrielle Roth, an American dancer and musician, on the basis of her knowledge of shamanism and trance-inducing dance techniques. It involves a wavelike sequence of body movements, passing through five phases characterized by the keywords: flowing, staccato, chaos, lyrical, and stillness. All of these stages have their appropriate rhythms. The method is now taught and practiced in many parts of the world.

Dance, like other art forms, has to steer a course between form and energy, structure and spontaneity, Apollonian order and Dionysiac passion. Different dance forms lean one way or the other, but if there is only Dionysiac force and ecstasy, divorced from any accepted conventions and floating in a rootless void, there can be no real beauty. Listen to the mindless background music in a supermarket or look at the crowd in a discotheque, jerking and twisting about like zombies, deafened by the noise. Sadly, you can witness the identical scene the world over. It's part of a one-size-fits-all culture, like the one-size-fits-all architecture that dominates the cities of the world. Apologists for this culture might say that's what people want, so we must give it to them. But if people go on buying synthetic white bread from their supermarket because that's the only kind on offer, it does not prove that they wouldn't buy something more nourishing if they were given the choice. The typical modern discotheque is a place of rootlessness. It is located in a nowhere, like the "nowhere man" of the Beatles song, whereas traditional folk dance, like all traditional culture, is located in a somewhere, and at the same time is linked with authentic cultures everywhere.

In folk dances one moves according to timeless patterns. Take the Scottish reels that I used to dance when I was growing up in Edinburgh or the north German dances that I learned later on. Typically there are four couples who start by facing each other forming a square, an age-old symbol of the earth and physical matter. They then dance in a circle, the symbol of heaven, perfection, and divinity. First the dancers go round clockwise then counterclockwise, and this also has a deeper significance, as clockwise and counterclockwise movements are woven into the universe. Seen from the perspective of the northern hemisphere, the diurnal movement of the sun is clockwise, while the monthly cycle of the moon is counterclockwise. And observe how the seeds of the sunflower are arranged in a double spiral, clockwise in one direction, counterclockwise in the other. The dancers then typically move in a criss-cross pattern, creating a cross within a circle, the solar cross of many mythologies, symbolizing the movement of the sun through the four seasons. Couples swing around arm in arm, dance away from each other, and then come together again in a beautiful moving harmony-in-polarity.

Fig. 11.8. Donate and myself in Weimar, 2006, during the New York Open Center Esoteric Quest in central Europe. In the background is Nicholas Goodrick-Clarke.

PHOTOGRAPH FROM THE AUTHOR'S COLLECTION

Another beautiful dance form with a cosmic dimension is the maypole dance, found in different variations in many countries of Europe as well as in North America. Traditionally performed on May Day, it features a pole or tree trunk with colored ribbons attached to the top end, and often surmounted by a crown or wreath of branches. The dancers, each one holding a ribbon, move around the pole in two directions (here again there is a clockwise and a counterclockwise movement), thus wrapping the ribbons around the tree in a spiraling, criss-cross pattern. If you look up the maypole dance on the internet, you will probably be told that it was originally a fertility ritual. This may be partly true—the phallic symbolism of the pole is obvious—but there are deeper layers of meaning here. The pole surely also represents the world tree, which in shamanic tradition marks the center of the world. Furthermore, in the old days these poles are said to have often been placed on geomantically charged spots.

So, what scornful people would write off as antiquated and rather comic turns out to be a well of profound symbolism and beauty. It is no coincidence that dancing is a common feature of paganism and neo-paganism worldwide. It is also an integral part of the ritual practice of the group in which my wife and I are both active. Dance is worship. It links us with Pan and the maenads in ancient Arcadia, with the Siberian shamans, the Native American sun dancers, and the English Morris dancers with their bells and ribbons. It is part of the fabric of being a Pagan.

12

Books, Travels, and Crises

The gods dwell wherever they are made welcome. We made them welcome in the home where we lived for twelve years in Bremen, first as tenants then as owners. It was a four-story terrace house in a 1960s housing development that was regarded as a model of post-war urban planning. The building was a marked contrast to the old Brandenburg house, but delightful nonetheless. There was a spacious living room with a broad balcony overlooking a garden that you entered from the basement. After a time we built a stair leading down to the garden from the balcony.

In the past I had made various attempts to create a sacred garden, and I had always moved on before the garden was complete. Now we set about transforming the Bremen garden into a sacred space. When we took it over it was basically a rectangle about forty feet long and twenty feet wide, rising slightly from the house with a raised bed at the back and straight flower beds on either side. According to basic feng shui principles the layout was all wrong. The energy simply shot through it in a straight line. In the middle was a rectangular lawn in very bad condition, which we almost never used.

We decided to give the garden a solar theme. As a focal point we had a sundial made, paid for as a generous wedding gift. It consisted of a block of sandstone with a working sundial on top and motifs carved into the sides to symbolize the four elements and the four compass directions: a tree for earth and north, a feather for air and east, flames for fire and south, and waves for water and west. I determined its position using a pendulum. The sundial was made by Frank Graupner, a momumental mason with a workshop close to the Riensberg cemetery in Bremen. Frank, who later became a good friend, was and is a real artist and craftsman, and the sundial he created is a work of art, which now stands in the garden of our present house. He inspired me to take up stone carving myself—but more about that later.

Fig. 12.1 The garden of our house in Bremen after we redesigned it according to basic geomantic principals.

PHOTOGRAPH BY THE AUTHOR

We then replaced the lawn with a paved area, greatly enlarging the flower beds and making the borders curved, so that the overall shape of the paving suggested a crescent moon. Now the energy, instead of shooting straight through the garden, swerved and undulated through it snakewise.

On the raised bed at the back and the south end of the garden we placed a large stone obelisk that I had acquired in Hamburg and taken with me to Rühstädt. According to the Roman writer Pliny the Elder, an obelisk represents a solidified ray of sunlight, so the southern position was appropriate. In the east for air we put a cast-iron statuette of a winged fairy, while in the west for water we placed a concrete urn filled with seashells, and Donate strung some more shells together and hung them from a pergola that we had built on the western side. Other features included a stone head of a Green Man that I had bought some years earlier from a dealer in England. There were also some fine mature trees that we left in place. In the small front garden by the main door of the house we placed a model of the Stone of Good Fortune at Goethe's Garden House in Weimar. All over the place Donate hung strings of glass prayer beads, shells, stones, and various other materials. We grew fond of the house itself as well. I had a spacious attic study, while Donate had her own study on the floor below. The living room was large enough for the Mondgarten meetings.

When we moved into the house I was sixty-one years old and had taken early retirement from UNESCO. Now I could devote more time to my writing as well as a certain amount of traveling and lecturing. In October 2005 I traveled to the Hague for a conference on Masonic and esoteric heritage. The morning after I returned home my brother David called me to say that during the night our father had died of kidney failure in a hospital in Edinburgh. He had reached the age of ninety-one and had been ailing for some time.

Fig. 12.2. Prayer beads in the form of shells,
placed by Donate in the west in our garden in Bremen.

PHOTOGRAPH BY DONATE MCINTOSH

I flew to Edinburgh and Donate joined me a couple of days later.
We stayed at a guest house in Colinton Road, right next door to
the house where J. K. Rowling then lived—something that pleased
Donate, as she was a great fan of the Harry Potter books. The service was held in the Canongate Chapel on the High Street and was
conducted by the Reverend Charles Robertson, a very warm and
likable man, who acted as chaplain to the royal family when they
stayed at nearby Holyrood Palace. The chapel was full of friends, colleagues, and family members from far and wide. I gave an address in

which I spoke of my father's many gifts, including a remarkable gift of friendship. He had a warmth and charm that brought him friends in many countries, so that, when I was planning a trip to a particular place, he would often say: "You must look up my friend so-and-so." Throughout my life he was always ready to give me loving help, support, and advice. The farewell to him was heart-wrenching but also heartwarming, with wonderful tributes from other members of the family and from the minister. While we were in Edinburgh I took Donate on a tour of the city in a rented car and showed her some of the places associated with my childhood, including our house in Blacket Place.

Looking back, I realize how much my parents contributed to my becoming a writer. Our house was full of books, including many novels by contemporary writers, so early on I had good models to follow. Already as a teenager I began to write short stories with my parents' encouragement, and over the years I also attempted novels, but initially without success. Then, after moving to Germany, I teamed up with my old college friend Tim Jeal and started work on a thriller based on a story that I had read in *Der Spiegel* about East German espionage in the West, using former inmates of the Lebensborn, a chain of maternity and children's homes run by the Nazi SS, partly for illegitimate children of women in the occupied countries. After the war many of these children landed in the German Democratic Republic, whose espionage service hit on the idea of using them as spies, with consequences that were often tragic. Our story moves between East and West Germany and Denmark. The cooperation worked well, with me doing most of the initial writing and Tim doing fine-tuning and sharing in the plotting and planning. As I had all kinds of other projects, it took us nine years altogether to complete the book. The initial title was *The Lebensborn Boy*. We secured an agent who sent it round the publishers, but they all turned it down ("Very good, but we can't make it work in the current market").

Eventually it came out under our own publishing imprint, which I shall come to in the next chapter.

Meanwhile I had started work translating Thomas Hakl's massive work on Eranos from German into English. The project was first mooted at the 2004 meeting of the Palladian Academy at the Domaine de Taurenne. It was agreed that I would translate some sample material, and Allison Coudert, then professor of religious studies at the University of California at Davis, offered to look for a publisher. She soon persuaded the firm of Equinox, based in England, to accept the book, and I started work. It was a herculean task, as the final printed version came to over four hundred pages of small print, and I had to juggle it with other assignments including a two-year return to my old job at the UNESCO Institute from 2006 to 2008. At the same time, translating the book taught me a great deal. Eranos was a unique project, created by a unique woman, Olga Fröbe-Kapteyn, and involved a galaxy of distinguished scholars that included Carl Gustav Jung, Gershom Scholem, Erich Neumann, Karl Kerenyi, Mircea Eliade, and Henry Corbin, to name only a few. What made Eranos special was that it was not just a scholarly enterprise but had a lot to do with the search for deeper spiritual meaning. Over the years it developed a kind of collective spirit, embodied in a stone stele inscribed with the words *"GENIO LOCI IGNOTO"* (To the unknown spirit of this place).

In his introduction Thomas Hakl writes as follows: "I cannot and will not deny that something stirred in me as I stood alone one day in the summer of 1998 in front of the famous stele in the garden of Eranos in Moscia-Ascona. . . . How many important people had already stood there like me, carrying their dreams, hopes and disappointments with them?" And of the purpose of Eranos he writes: "The search for our spiritual roots, the intuitive knowledge of a common transcendental origin of humankind, and the corresponding longing for a 'return' to what in religious language is called the 'divine'—all of this seemed to me to constitute the deeper connecting motivation that sustained the Eranos project for so many decades."[1] The book is subtitled "an alternative intellectual history of the 20th century," and to read it is a rich experience.

There are certain parallels between Eranos and the New Age Esalen Institute in California, which I was privileged to visit in May 2006, when I took part in a seminar there at the invitation of Michael Murphy, who had cofounded Esalen on a family property at Big Sur in the early 1960s. The seminar, which was on the theme of the interface between esotericism and fiction, brought together an international group of scholars that included Wouter Hanegraaff, Marco Pasi, Antoine Faivre, Jean-Pierre Brach, and Arthur Versluis. Several other participants and I gathered at a motel near the San Francisco airport where we were met by Walter Tanner of the Esalen staff, and we set off in a minibus down the Pacific coast via Highway 1. After a drive of about three and a half hours we came to an inconspicuous turning where a wooden sign said: "Esalen Institute by Reservation Only." A dirt driveway led down to what I can best describe as a kind of Shangri-La. The whole complex, including the original house of the estate and various other buildings, is spread out along the top of a line of cliffs plunging down to a wave-battered, rocky shore. Everywhere is abundant greenery: eucalyptus and pine trees, acanthus bushes, lawns and acres of vegetable and flower gardens. On the landward side, beyond the highway, huge condors wheel lazily over a range of green hills.

Murphy and the cofounder of Esalen, Richard Price, had a powerful vision that was in many ways similar to the one that motivated Olga Fröbe-Kapteyn in the creation of Eranos. Both projects involved the bringing together of different spiritual paths, inner traditions and esoteric currents of both East and West, and both encompassed systematic scholarship and research as well as the promotion of inner development. Esalen's mission has always had to do with the furthering of "human potential," a phrase referring to Aldous Huxley's view that we humans generally use only 10 percent of the immense potential that we possess. At Esalen the effort to expand human potential has encompassed not only religion but also psychology, parapsychology, psychotherapy, massage, dance, ecology, diet, and more.

One of the most pioneering achievements of Esalen was the role that it played, from the 1960s on, in opening up new relations with Russia through visits, exchanges, and shared research projects, especially in the area of parapsychology. A high point of this collaboration came in 1989 when Esalen sponsored a visit to the United States by Boris Yeltsin, already a prominent politician and soon to be elected president of the Russian Republic. A key moment in the visit was when Yeltsin was taken to a Randalls grocery store in Houston, Texas, and was so bowled over by the array of goods and the low prices that he returned to Russia minus the last vestige of Bolshevism that he had possessed. Thus Esalen made its own contribution to ending Russian communism and the Cold War, and has had an important impact on American culture and society in the modern age.

In the same year as my Esalen visit I was called back temporarily to the UNESCO Institute in Hamburg, following the sudden departure of my successor and pending the engagement of a new head of publications. For the next two years I had a strenuous routine, commuting by train between Bremen and Hamburg and doing my old job, which involved two visits to Africa in connection with a book series on African adult education. These I was able to combine with visiting Lionel and Lynn at their house in Simon's Town near Cape Town. With what little time and energy I had left over I continued collaborating with Tim Jeal writing what eventually became *The Lebensborn Spy*. This hectic period came to an end in 2008, when I finally left the UNESCO Institute.

In the autumn of 2009, out of sunny skies came a big thunderbolt. Until then it had been a full and exciting year. Together we made a trip to Edinburgh, arranged the sale of the Rühstädt house, attended a midsummer gathering at the Externsteine, held our seasonal Mondgarten rituals, and cultivated our garden. I went on with my translation and writing work, gave my English classes at the university, attended a meeting of the Palladian Academy at Taurenne, and from there went on to Strasbourg for a conference of the European Society for the Study of Western Esotericism (ESSWE).

In August Donate went into hospital in Bremen for an operation on her right knee to correct the angle of the joint. It went well and she came out after a week, then had a slow convalescence. She had a lot of pain from the operation and very limited mobility and had to use crutches. Just when she was beginning to get back to normal from the operation she began to suffer from severe headaches and impaired vision in her right eye. Her eye doctor and neurologist were baffled. Finally she was given a referral to the Eastern Hospital in Bremen to have further tests. She had the ill luck to check in at the beginning of a weekend when no tests were being done, and had to wait in a lot of pain until Monday when she was given a scan, which revealed a small tumor behind the right eye, pressing against the pituitary gland, which in turn was pressing against the optic nerve.

Two days later, having been transferred to the Central Hospital in Bremen, she was operated on by the head neurosurgeon Dr. Neubauer, to remove the tumor. He telephoned me afterward to say that the operation had gone well. Nine days later she came home, but the following day Dr. Neubauer phoned to say that the tumor had turned out to be malignant and that she would have to undergo further tests and treatment. Over the next few days I took her three times to the hospital for tests and scans. One Sunday the members of our Mondgarten circle held a supporting ritual from their own homes, lighting candles at a prearranged time. Donate made a lovely altar in the living room, with flowers, candles, and a cloth with a rose pattern. We meditated for about forty minutes, sensing the others joining in at a distance, and Donate said that she could feel when one of them began to chant. Afterward she felt very soothed and strengthened.

The next four weeks were a grim time. Four different laboratories specializing in brain tumors carefully analyzed the material and came to the joint conclusion that it was an extremely rare and malignant type of tumor. It seemed like an ineluctable death sentence. The tumor turned out to be an extremely rare kind that usually only occurs in children. Worldwide there were only about twenty-one other cases of it occurring in adults, and it was a very difficult challenge for the doctors to determine the right treatment. Consultations between them went back and forth between Bremen, Berlin, and elsewhere. Finally a course of chemotherapy was decided upon, which was carried out in three phases in a rather gloomy, Dickensian ward of the Central Hospital. It was a terrible ordeal for Donate, and when she came home after the third phase of treatment she was so weak that she had to stay in bed for several weeks and could take only semiliquid food. She could not walk or even stand up, and could only speak in a whisper, as the cytostatic drugs had attacked her vocal chords. She had a small bell by her bedside so that she could call me at any time. Her general practitioner came regularly to check her progress. I nursed her as best I could, and gradually over several months she got her strength back. Then came a course of radiotherapy, which she received as an outpatient, taking a taxi to the clinic every day. At the end of six weeks further tests showed, to our enormous relief and against all expectations, that the impossible had happened: the tumor had been destroyed. Donate's doctors called her "a walking miracle."

The main thing that sustained her during this ordeal was her inner contact with the great Goddess, combined with many decades of working with the subtle levels of the body. During meditation she received a message that the Goddess was giving her a task to carry out when she recovered and that the task involved writing, so she knew she would not die. She was also strengthened by the sense that many friends and family members, to whom she had sent emails before going into hospital, were sending her their love and support, which she visualized as many golden threads that the Goddess wove into a huge golden sphere. Feeling herself being inside and protected in this sphere added much to support her self-healing capacities.

After the treatment was over there began a long period of recovery, which included five weeks in a convalescent clinic at Soltau in the Lüneburg Heath, where she had a pleasant, spacious room and could go for walks in the nearby woods. There were lots of tiresome aftereffects of the chemotherapy, but gradually she was able to return to a relatively normal life.

In fulfillment of the task she had been given by the Goddess, she set about putting together a beautiful collection of ritual songs in German, many of them translated by her from English originals. The texts of the songs were accompanied by musical notes provided by the composer Sylke Zimpel. Donate provided a detailed and searching introduction to the collection, with her reflections on nature religion, the symbolism of the elements, and the role of music, song, and rhythm in ritual. This collection was something entirely new in Germany and was published to great acclaim in 2011 by Christel Göttert Verlag.

By the summer of 2010, following Donate's convalescence, we had resumed our busy round of activities, with Mondgarten rituals, additions to the garden, work on our respective writing projects, and meetings of my folk dance group. In July, as was our custom at that time, we had a holiday on the island of Langeoog off the North Sea coast, along with Janna and her friend Sylvia, as well as Julia, Jan, and their daughters Clara and Anna. Langeoog, once the home of the singer Lale Andersen (well known for "Lili Marleen"), is an idyll, preserved as in a time warp, with its unspoiled beaches, its undulating dunes, and its little toytown railway connecting the harbor with the pretty, well-kept town. One afternoon we went to a sing-along in a natural amphitheater in the dunes where about four hundred people had gathered. Accompanied by two accordionists, we sang folk songs and sea shanties that took me back to the pub in St. Pauli and the "singing landlady." My schedule that year also included teaching at a seminar in the esoteric studies program at Exeter, and attending Nicholas and Clare Goodrick-Clarke's silver wedding celebration in Oxford.

I also spent a weekend in Berlin taking part in a Stav workshop. Stav is a kind of Nordic tai chi, based on the runes, which was developed by the Norwegian Ivar Hafskjold, partly out of a traditional fighting system preserved, as he claimed, in his family over many generations, and partly on the basis of martial arts techniques that he learned during a fourteen-year sojourn in Japan. The core of the system is a series of body postures based on the sixteen runes of the Younger *Futhark*, the later runic alphabet, created in about the eighth century CE. These can be used simply as yoga positions or as martial arts movements. For over twenty years now I have practiced the Stav positions every morning and find them very beneficial to health, posture, and general vitality. In addition Stav posits a social hierarchy composed of five classes or estates, namely *konge* (king), *herse* (warrior), *jarl* (nobleman), *karl* (yeoman), and *trel* (serf). These are not written in stone, and one can move from one class to another, depending on one's abilities. Each has its own martial arts movements, but one can decide to use the movement of a class other than one's own if the situation calls for it. For example, if an enemy rushes toward you wielding a weapon, you can make the warrior's move and attack them head-on, or you can do what the serf would do, namely step sideways and let the attacker rush past, and it may sometimes be wiser to do the latter.

This is of course a variation on the ancient Indo-European tripartite class system, identified by the French philologist and scholar of religion Georges Dumézil (1898–1986) comprising (a) rulers/priests,

Fig. 12.3. Practicing the Stav martial arts system in Berlin with instructor Graham Butcher. See also color plate 9.

PHOTOGRAPH FROM THE AUTHOR'S COLLECTION

(b) warriors, and (c) commoners (peasants and tradespeople). This system, in different forms, spread all over the Indo-European world, and I have observed certain traces of it in Germany today in the form of the *Stände* (estates). Whereas in England a cobbler would probably think of himself as belonging to the working class, in Germany he would be more likely to consider himself a member of the estate of shoemakers with a certificate to prove it, and would have a certain pride in that status. Similarly there is an estate of the stonemasons, the lawyers, the farmers, the chimney sweeps, and so on. This system is of course gradually being eroded, but it is still noticeable. While a system of estates has its abuses, as in certain aspects of the tradition of the Hindu castes, in a moderate form it has much to commend it. Ideally it would mean that each person would fulfill the role in society to which they were suited by temperament and ability, and that they would be respected accordingly—unlike in modern society, where too many people are encouraged to think that they should aim for an estate to which they are not suited, resulting in many square pegs in round holes and much frustration.

13

Aspects of Mercury and Odin

While I was living in New York in the 1990s I consulted an astrologer who practiced the Vedic system of astrology, according to which one's life is divided into planetary periods. He told me that I was about to enter a Mercury period that would last for fourteen years. Mercury is, among other things, the planet of communication, language, speech, writing, and the quality of versatility. It is strong in my natal horoscope and has always stood me in good stead. Moreover the Romans considered Odin or Wotan to be the northern equivalent of Mercury, so it is not surprising that, when I turned to the Nordic mysteries, Odin came to have a special meaning for me. The prediction about my Mercury period seemed to be confirmed by the job that I took on at the UNESCO Institute in Hamburg. I was using several languages—English, French, German, Russian, and even a bit of Spanish, which I had studied for a semester. The job included being an editor, public relations officer, writer, and head of a publications department—all very mercurial. I started there in 1994 and, after an absence and a second stint of two years, finally left in 2008, as I mentioned earlier—a period of exactly fourteen years, including the coming and going in between. My astrologer friend had been spot-on. The only trouble was that the job monopolized the mercurial part of my mind, allowing me very little time or energy to use it for my deeper interests. That changed when I finally retired from the Institute and apparently a different sort of Mercury period began.

After I left the Institute I would occasionally pay a visit there, and in June 2011 I attended a farewell reception for Adama Ouane, the second director under whom I had worked. At one point there had been a certain amount of friction between us, but I came to have great admiration for him. A native of Mali, he had studied for nine years in Russia and was fluent in Russian as well as numerous other languages including English, French, and German. The farewell party was a moving event. I gave a speech in which I recalled my time at the Institute, saying that, in all the time I had worked in the United Nations system, Adama was the most outstanding boss I had known and I wished to thank him for his inspiration and leadership. He was very moved and came forward to embrace me.

My mercurial life continued and included a fair amount of travel and lecturing. One trip to the United States in February of 2011 involved an unusually full program. I flew to New York and stayed for a couple of nights in Bayonne, New Jersey, with my friends Piers Vaughan and Jason Sheridan. A couple of days later I moved to a hotel on Broadway and in the evening had dinner at the invitation of my friend David Lindez at the Players Club on Gramercy Park, the square where my mother had grown up. After dinner we walked over to the building where her family's apartment had been. The doorman showed us the entrance hall, which was decorated with beautiful marble tiles. I had been there many years earlier at the age of nineteen, and it was a nostalgic experience seeing it again. The next day I gave a lecture on Rosicrucianism at the Masonic Center on Twenty-Third Street and signed copies of my two latest books. From New York I traveled by train to upstate New York state to stay a couple of nights with Joscelyn Godwin at Hamilton and give a lecture to his Western esotericism class at Colgate University. Then it was down to Washington, DC, where I stayed with my old friends Lisa and Clyde in Cleveland Park. Marion Redd joined me there and attended a lecture on sacred gardens that I gave at the Washington Masonic Memorial building in Alexandria, Virginia. While in Washington I organized a family lunch at a diner on Connecticut Avenue. June, Terry, and their daughter Fiona came. So did my cousin Bill Bainbridge with his wife, Marcia, and my other cousin John Bainbridge with his partner, Barbara. Then June drove me to their house in Mercersberg, Pennsylvania, where I spent a night before flying home from Dulles airport.

I was now in my late sixties, when many men in retirement spend their days puttering aimlessly about. That was not for me. The years were fuller than ever with all kinds of activities: seasonal rituals of Langhus and Mondgarten, sessions of our folk dancing group, courses in Plattdeutsch, holidays on Langeoog, seminars at Exeter, lecture trips to the United States, Palladian Academy meetings, esoteric quests, completion of the Eranos translation, the sale of our house in Rühstädt, continuing work on the Lebensborn thriller, and much more.

A big event of 2011 was Donate's sixtieth birthday in November. As it came so soon after her surviving the brain tumor she called it her re-birthday. We held a lunch party for many family members and friends at Höpkens Ruh, a beautiful hotel set in a park in the Bremen district of Oberneuland. I had put together a photograph album showing different phases of her life, and the pictures were also presented in a slide show with a running commentary by Donate. There was a magnificent birthday cake decorated with marzipan poppies (the poppy being her favorite flower), which was wheeled in with candles lit and fireworks blazing. Everyone sang a song in her honor, composed by family members. I gave a speech and unveiled a portrait of her that I had painted.

Another important birthday was my seventieth in September 2013, which Donate and I celebrated with a big lunch party at the Park Hotel in Bremen for family and friends of us both, among them my two sons who gave a great speech in my honor, involving an alphabetical list of the things they associated with me. Some of the guests came from far and wide. My old school friend David McDougall was one whom I had not seen for about thirty years. He came three days early, and I met him at Bremen airport. We had supper together near his hotel and immediately our old friendship was resumed. Next day our mutual school friend Iain Taylor arrived by train from Berlin. In the intervening years Iain had led a most unusual life. As a schoolboy he had become a convinced communist, and after studying at Glasgow University, he had emigrated to Poland and got a job with a state publishing house in Warsaw as an editor and English translator. Then, after the collapse of communism, I heard that he was living in Berlin. David McDougall, who had been in touch with him, gave me his contact details, and I called him and arranged to meet him for dinner at a Berlin restaurant. It was nearly forty years since we had last met, but our friendship immediately sparked again as though those years had never passed. Also attending the birthday party were Lionel and Lynn, who were on their way to England from South Africa and were able to make a side trip to Bremen for the event.

The year 2013 was also the fiftieth anniversary of the first meeting of the Anonymous Society of Writers, which I had cofounded at Oxford, and I felt that it should be celebrated. I contacted as many of the old members as I could, and we arranged to have a reunion lunch in London at a Turkish restaurant called Tas in Great Russell Street near the British Museum. Frederick Turner came over from the States and was able to combine the visit with a lecture assignment at our old college, Christ Church. Also present, apart from myself, were Tim Jeal, cofounder of the society; John Penycate, who, after a distinguished career in television, had become a lecturer on cruise

Fig. 13.1. Members of the Anonymous Society of Writers meeting for lunch at the Tas restaurant in Bloomsbury, London, in about 2013. *Left to right*: David Lumb, Frederick Turner, John Penycate, Christopher McIntosh, James Gordon, Tim Jeal, Barney Powell.

PHOTOGRAPH FROM THE AUTHOR'S COLLECTION

ships; Barney Powell, who had worked in banking in the Far East; Richard Johnstone, an oil industry expert; and James Gordon, who had pursued a many-faceted career in popular music, race relations, teaching, and local politics. At subsequent meetings we were joined by David Lumb, who had been a teacher and then an educational consultant. The first reunion was such fun that we decided to repeat it, and up to now we have continued to meet every year.

That autumn of 2013 I also wrote a short memoir about Ian Hamilton Finlay, using a mass of material relating to him that I had collected over the years: publications of his Wild Hawthorn Press, correspondence with me and others, small prints of his poems and images, books and articles about him, catalogs of his exhibitions, and other material including Katherine's fine doctoral thesis about him.

But I asked myself whether he would have wanted me to write such a memoir. It was October of 2013, and our Mondgarten group was about to celebrate Halloween, which is the festival when one remembers the dead or seeks to communicate with them. In the room where we held the ritual I placed a photograph of Ian on a table. During the part of the ritual that took the form of a meditation I tried to put myself in touch with him and ask him what he thought about the memoir project. The message I got was that if anyone could write a suitable memoir it was me. I went ahead with the project and got in touch with Ian's ex-wife Sue Swan and his son Alec, both of whom read the text and gave me important feedback. So *Ian Hamilton Finlay: A Memoir* was duly published in 2014, under the Vanadis imprint that Donate and I and our friend Judith Kraus had started together.

The year 2014 was also the four-hundredth anniversary of the publication of the *Fama Fraternitatis*, the first of three Rosicrucian manifestos and one of the key works of the Western esoteric tradition, first published in German in 1614 and in a very defective English translation in 1652. Donate and I decided to produce a new translation and publish it under the Vanadis imprint to mark the anniversary. It came out in June of 2014 and was well received. Our translation, still on the market, was included in an edition of all three manifestos published by Weiser Books, with translations of the second and third manifestos by Joscelyn Godwin.[1] We also published a modern German translation by Donate.

Having done much translation over the years from German, French, and Russian, I know that there is much truth in the Italian saying *"traduttore, traditore"* (the translator is a traitor). This applies also to the translation programs that one finds on the internet. A UNESCO colleague of mine related a case where someone, to test one such program, translated the biblical saying "the spirit is willing, but the flesh is weak" into Russian and then back into English, and what came out at the end was: "The vodka is good, but the meat is rotten." There were mistakes almost as bad as that in the 1652 translation of the *Fama* and in some of the so-called translations that I have had to deal with as an editor.

Two more books came out under the Vanadis imprint in 2014. One was a volume of short stories by me entitled *Master of the Starlit Grove*. The title was also that of the main story—actually a novella—about a young man's journey to paganism and his discovery of a pagan egregore that had kept paganism half-covertly alive over the centuries until the time was ripe for its revival. The other Vanadis book that came out at that time was the novel *The Lebensborn Boy*, which I had written together with Tim Jeal. It was published under the joint pseudonym of Roy Havelland. Later I revised the book and in 2017, with Tim's agreement, published a second edition under my own name with the title *The Lebensborn Spy*, which is still on the market. The book is not simply a thriller but a story about a clash of values, contrasting the "nowhere" world of Marxist ideology with the "somewhere" world of a Danish island. For those who can read between the lines there is also a subtle pagan message.

In the spring of 2014 I spent several delightful days in Thomas Hakl's esoteric library in Graz. Thomas had decided to create a written memorial to the library by commissioning various of his friends to write scholarly essays broadly based on material in the collection. The resulting texts were to appear in four volumes, published in English, German, French, and Italian respectively.[2] I opted to write on the theme of paganism as reflected in the library, adopting a rather random approach that cut across several different categories of the collection—psychology, folklore, mythology, fiction, history of religion, and so on. The task was a magical experience from the moment of entering the Octagon, as the building is called on account of its shape. The approach from the house to the library annex is via a mysterious corridor and a black sliding door decorated with a

Chinese Taoist character in gold leaf, giving one the sense that one is entering a sanctum—perhaps a modern equivalent of the vault of Christian Rosenkreuz, which was said to contain a universal compendium of knowledge. It was a privilege to spend long hours browsing the collection, interspersed with many fascinating conversations with Thomas and with Hereward Tilton, my former colleague in the Exeter program, who was working on an essay on the Golden and Rosy Cross Order.

The year continued pleasantly with another reunion of Donate's relatives, a school graduation ceremony for my grandson Daniel, a Mondgarten midsummer celebration, a trip to England for me, and a stunning World Cup final game in Brazil ending in a 1–0 victory for Germany over Argentina. Then out of the blue came a thunderbolt. Walking with Donate in the Rhododendron Park in Bremen, I suddenly felt weak and wobbly and had to sit down immediately on a bench. Next day I went to see my general practitioner, Dr. Neumann-Kittler, who did a few tests and then said that I needed to see a heart specialist without delay. He arranged an appointment for 12:30 the next day at the Red Cross Hospital in Bremen. I went there with Donate and was given more tests including an electrocardiogram. Result: I had recently had a mild heart attack without realizing it at the time, as part of the heart was not pumping as it should. I was given an appointment to go back in five days for more intensive tests.

In the meantime our Mondgarten group held a meeting to celebrate the late summer festival of Lammas. Beforehand Donate asked me if I wished the ritual to address any particular deity, and I chose the three Norns, the goddesses of fate, Urd, Verdandi, and Skuld, representing past, present, and future. I printed out a nineteenth-century engraving of the Norns from the internet and had it on the table in our living room during the ritual. Skuld was portrayed with her face half covered by a veil—but only half, as the future can only be partly foreseen. I was contemplating this image when Donate spoke of the need for trust. I found the combination of her words and the image curiously calming and reassuring.

Back at the hospital three days later I was given a more intensive test involving the insertion of a catheter through a vein in my right arm and up to the heart. The conclusion was that some of the coronary arteries were severely narrowed or blocked. I was going to need a major operation involving three bypasses and would be in hospital for about ten days. While I was waiting for the operation appointment I had a visit from Jörg, who brought me a heart-shaped piece of rose quartz that he had charged with three runes: Algiz for protection, Eihwaz for strength and flexibility, Fehu for energy. He came back again the next day and we went to a nearby café, where we talked about the subject of death and the Nordic tradition of the *fylgja*, one's companion spirit, which is normally invisible but will sometimes appear, usually as a sign that one is near to death. Jörg told me that he had recently made contact with his *fylgja*, whom he saw as a radiant young woman, holding out her hands to welcome him—prematurely, as it was to be many years before he died.

Next day I went into the hospital for the operation. It was early September. On my bedside table I had Jörg's crystal and a sort of cardboard easel that I had made with the Norns on one side and Odin on the other. I was knocked out with a full anesthetic at about 10 a.m. on a Friday and did not wake up until around midnight. My first thought was: Well, I'm alive! I spent Saturday in intensive care, linked up to all kinds of tubes, wires, and monitors. That night I got very little sleep, as I had an air bag around my left arm, which inflated every hour, gripping the arm tightly while a monitoring device measured the blood pressure. By Sunday morning I was starting to feel better, and could stand up and walk to the bathroom. On that day or the next I was transferred to a regular ward where I stayed for another few days before going home. Donate had visited me regularly and helped to keep my spirits up. I also had visits from Jörg and from my son Angus and daughter-in-law Susan. There followed a period of three weeks as an outpatient at a rehabilitation clinic, then it was more or less back to a normal life, except that from then on I had to take a battery of pills every day. Also, as recommended, I started to go once a week to a group fitness class, led by a physiotherapist.

My health problems were not yet over. Having had no serious illness in my life up to the heart attack, I now entered a period of several months when I was in and out of hospital with various tiresome complaints. One Friday morning in December I collapsed in the kitchen with dizziness and nausea and was taken off in an ambulance to the Saint Josef hospital in Bremen, where I was treated for a malfunction of the inner ear. On the second or third night in the ward I had a powerful dream. I was in an old city—I think it was Paris—where I was led through the streets by a young, dark-haired woman. She took me to an underground place where there was a sacred spring with healing water, rather thick and yellow, that came out of a well, which was attended by a young man. At first I hesitated to drink from the well, thinking that it might have associations of too Christian a character. Then the thought came to me that it was much older than Christianity and belonged to the Earth Goddess, so I drank some of the water. After that I sat in an alcove at a table until another man came up and asked me if he could sit there. I then went outside again with the dark woman, and we came to a place where a stream ran parallel to a street. There was a rainbow-shaped stone bridge over the stream. The bridge had no walls or railing. I saw that the dark-haired woman was already on the other side. I hesitated, then walked safely across. At that point I woke up.

When I recounted the dream to Donate she suggested that the dark-haired woman was the Dark Goddess or Skuld, the third Norn, who is guardian of the realm of death. A Jungian analyst would probably say that the woman was my anima, one of Jung's "archetypes," the inherited motifs that he believed to be lodged in the collective unconscious. Her male counterpart, the animus, would be represented in my case by Odin/Mercury. For Jung, dreams are pointers to what he called "individuation," the process of integrating the contrasting parts of oneself into one harmonious pattern, comparable to the mandalas of Asiatic tradition, of which he created many versions of his own.

For me, dream interpretation is a kind of archaeology, an excavation that may reveal many layers. On one level I see the dark woman of my dream as a psychopomp, one who brings new souls into incarnation and accompanies them into the celestial realm at death. At the time of the dream I had recently had my heart operation and was now in hospital again with another health problem. The theme of mortality was not far from my thoughts, and the river that featured in the dream was a classic symbol of the boundary between life and death. The dreamt experience of being led across the bridge by the dark woman was distinctly calming and reassuring, like Jörg's vision of his *fylgja* in the form of a fair-haired woman opening her arms to him. As for the motif of the spring, this is of course a universal archetype. It is the wellspring of life at the center of the garden of paradise, the source of the vital element water, the fountain of fate at the foot of the World Tree, and much else.

This was not my only vision of a goddess figure linked with the theme of water. Different variations of the goddess have featured over the years in my dreams, in my fiction, and in my art. I painted a particularly vivid image of her in 1992 while I was living in New York and having a course of psychotherapy from a young woman who approached therapy from the Buddhist point of view. She encouraged me to translate my dreams and visions into pictures, and this was one of the results. A radiant woman, with a headdress of leaves and flowers, is standing by a pool in a landscape of woods and mountains. Around her are various symbols of the elements: an owl for air, a dragon for fire, fish for water, and a cave in the bank for the depths of the earth.

Fig. 13.2. Goddess of the Elements, painted by me in 1992.
See also color plate 10.

While this would all make sense in Jungian terms, there are surely some visions and dreams whose purpose is not merely to help the individual dreamer toward self-integration but which are messages from our forebears that teach us something about our collective situation, where we have come from as human beings and where we may be going. If we excavate the deeper strata of certain dreams we come to a level that is best expressed by the German word *uralt*, meaning something between "primal" and "age-old." And what of the Parisian setting in the dream? Paris, with its boulevards, quays, palaces, towers, cafés, and picture-postcard vistas, was like a veneer covering those older layers underneath. Below Hausmann's grand thoroughfares, below the remains of the medieval city, below Roman Paris, below even the settlement of the Parisii tribe, I found the well of the Earth Goddess. I feel the nineteenth-century poet Algernon Charles Swinburne might have been inspired by a similar dream when he wrote his poem "Hertha" (the name being that of the Germanic earth goddess):

> *I am that which began, out of me the years roll,*
> *Out of me God and man, I am equal and whole.*

Another English poet, Robert Graves, believed in an ancient goddess who was the inspiration for all true poetry. In his book *The White Goddess*, he wrote: "My thesis is that the language of poetic myth anciently current in the Mediterranean and Northern Europe was a magical language bound up with popular religious ceremonies in honor of the Moon-Goddess, or Muse, some of them from the Old Stone Age, and that this remains the language of true poetry. . . ."[3] Graves spoke of the Moon Goddess, whereas in my dream it was the Earth Goddess who appeared. One can treat these two either as separate deities or as different aspects of one universal Goddess. The moon is associated with the element water, the tides, the female menstrual cycle, pregnancy and the amniotic fluid, dreams, visions, moods and—if Graves is right—poetic inspiration. The moon also speaks of the otherworldly, whereas the Earth is the planet itself, the fertile soil, the foundation of life and of nature, the piece of land to which we belong, the qualities of rootedness and practicality. Much of my own life has been marked by the endeavor to balance and combine these two realms.

14

In the Footsteps of the Old Ones

Earlier I quoted Joseph Campbell's remark about the gods being alive on the corner of Broadway and Forty-Second Street—a corner that I used to pass nearly every day on the bus route between the United Nations and my home on the Upper West Side. I confess that I wasn't looking out for gods at that time, but there may have been a few in disguise amid the bustling crowd, the neon lights, and the razzle-dazzle, and who knows what one might encounter if one were to go down below the street level, as I did in my dream when I descended below the streets of Paris. There are other places where the gods are very much above the surface and thriving. This is the case in many of the countries of eastern Europe, such as Latvia, which Donate and I visited in April 2015 for the fifth conference of the European Society for the Study of Esotericism, held at the University of Riga. During our stay we contacted Sandra, who had been in our folk dance group in Bremen and had in the meantime married and had a small son. She and her husband Janiš showed us some photographs of their wedding, which was celebrated according to Latvian pagan tradition. The bride wore a crown of flowers, which was replaced by a headband when the marriage was sealed, then she threw the crown to an unmarried girl as a good luck charm for finding a husband. At one point they passed under an arch formed by the symbol of Jumis, god of fertility, agriculture, and well-being, decorated with oak branches for strength.

We soon discovered how ubiquitous the pagan tradition is in everyday Latvian life. The symbols of the gods are seen on the facades of houses, on household crockery, on items of jewelry, and woven into fabrics. In addition to Jumis, the most familiar gods include:

Dievs, the supreme deity, father of the gods, and the essence of all of them. Hence the modern pagan movement in Latvia is called Dievturi. The name is cognate with the Latin *deus*.

Mara, the great mother goddess, protectress of women, mothers, and children, and also goddess of the hearth and guardian of the land, the waters and all living things.

Laima, goddess of destiny, who decides whether one's life will be long or short, prosperous or poor, carefree or difficult.

Jānis, god of the summer solstice. His midsummer celebration, June 23, is the most important festival of the year for Latvians.

Ūsiņš, god of horses, bees, and light—a curious but beautiful and evocative trio.

In the neighboring country of Lithuania we would have found many similar god names and sigils. Among these, and in the folk customs and art of the region, one can find traces of an ancient goddess-centered religion that extended over a wide area of central and southeastern Europe, as has been shown by the great Lithuanian archaeologist and anthropologist Marija Gimbutas (1921–1994). She called this area Old Europe. On the basis of archaeological evidence she showed how its peaceful, sedentary, agriculture-based, goddess-worshipping, matriarchal culture was invaded from about 3000 BCE by a warlike, seminomadic, Indo-European people from the East, who introduced patriarchy, domesticated horses, the bow and arrow, fortifications, and their own pantheon, in which a male god reigned supreme.

Gimbutas portrays the culture of Old Europe as a prosperous, peaceful, well-ordered world where women had the leading role, but where both sexes lived in mutual respect. She presents this as proof that such a society is possible, and she makes her case very persuasively. So, do I regret the passing of her Old European matriarchal civilization? Yes and no. Yes, in the same way that I regret the decline of the basically decent, stable, tolerant, livable Britain that I grew up in. But then again, no, because I do not live in southeast Europe in 3000 BCE. I live in northern Germany in the twenty-first century, and I have made the choice to follow the ancient, Indigenous religion of northern Europe, since that is my spiritual heritage. I can accept her scenario of the clash between the two cultures, and I would argue that a reasonable entente between them was developed in the north. In the Nordic mythology there are two groups of gods, the Aesir and the Vanir, who would correspond respectively to the gods of the wandering Indo-European invaders and those of the settled goddess-worshippers. It must be remembered that Freya, who belonged to the Vanir, went to live with the Aesir and it was she who taught Odin the form of magic known as *seidh*. In this way and in others the feminine principle is given its due place in the Nordic world, and the sagas and epic poems are full of strong, determined female figures.

By now the reader will have gained some understanding of the stages that led me to the pagan way. As I have said earlier, I found it fulfilling on several different levels. However, being a Pagan had certain drawbacks, one being the lack of the kind of institutional basis that other religions have, including professional clergy who, apart from conducting services, can provide spiritual counseling or what in English is called "care of souls" (in German, *Seelsorge*). There have often been times of depression or crisis in my life when I have felt the need of spiritual and moral support from a fellow Pagan—I mean not simply the kind of support that a sympathetic friend would give, but the kind requiring special insight, knowledge, and empathy. In some countries this kind of support does exist among pagan communities. A good example is Britain, where, thanks largely to the work of the Pagan Federation, there are now pagan life counselors, hospital visitors, and prison visitors. The situation is similar in the United States, where there are even accredited college courses in spiritual counselling for Pagans. In Iceland too the Pagans are well provided with access to counseling. In Germany, however, the situation is bleaker. A hospital patient who makes a request for *Seelsorge* will be asked whether they are Catholic or Protestant or perhaps Muslim. The notion that someone might need something called pagan *Seelsorge* is usually met with blank incomprehension, at least in my experience.

I discussed this with Donate and with some of our pagan friends, and we decided to attempt the creation of a pagan spiritual counseling service in Germany. We formed a working group involving members of various different pagan affiliations, and soon discovered that we had bitten off a difficult and complicated task with many ifs and buts. What name should we use? How should we describe ourselves? Should we avoid dealing with psychotic or seriously mentally disturbed people? If not, how should we limit our target group? Should we confine ourselves to one help session? If not, how many? How should we insure ourselves against complaints from dissatisfied recipients of our help? What kind of qualifications should our helpers have? What should be the procedure for recording each case? Would there be issues of data protection? Over a series of meetings in Bremen, Berlin, and elsewhere we thrashed out these questions, drew up a set of procedures, and were ready to start. We settled on the name Verdandihilfe (Verdandi Help) after the second of the three Norns of time and fate—Urd, Verdandi, and Skuld—corresponding to past, present, and future or to the beginning, middle, and end of a process. We announced ourselves as widely as we could and waited to be inundated by calls for help, but only one came and then no more. Regretfully, we decided that in Germany the time was not ripe for Verdandihilfe and put the whole project on ice. However, we still have the written record of the system we put together, and perhaps one day we or some of our pagan friends will revive it.

Plate 1. An oil painting that I produced at about age twenty-one, following a dream in which I saw Pan leading a procession of maenads.

Plate 2. A *dol hareubang* (spirit of fertility) in the grounds of the Palace of Shining Happiness, Seoul.

PHOTOGRAPH BY THE AUTHOR

Plate 3. The author with a satyr in Thieles' Garden, Bremerhaven.
PHOTOGRAPH BY DONATE MCINTOSH

Plate 4. *Pan and Psyche*: a painting by Edward Burne-Jones, 1872.

Plate 5. Hilmar Örn ilmarsson conducting a kind of Asatru baptism ceremony or Julius Samúelsson. The boy is Julius's son Thorvaldur. In the background, *left to right*: Ólafur Sigurdsson, Lara Jóna horsteinsdóttir, Janna Kristín Berg.
PHOTOGRAPH BY THE AUTHOR

Plate 6. Donate drumming in our garden in Bremen.
PHOTOGRAPH BY THE AUTHOR

Plate 7. Helping to make a wreath of corn and roses during a midsummer ritual at our home in 2013.

Plate 8. The Langhus Morris dancing group in the garden of our house in Bremen.

Plate 9. Practicing the Stav martial arts system in Berlin
with instructor Graham Butcher.

Plate 10.
Goddess of
the Elements,
painted by me
in 1992.

Plate 11. The Runic Circle in our garden in Lilienthal. It is dedicated to the Norns, the three Nordic goddesses of time and fate.

Plate 12. A stele to the god Pan on our terrace in Lilienthal.

Plate 13. Prayer beads placed on the terrace by Donate.

Plate 14. Plaster relief of a maenad, surrounded by a trompe l'oeil frame.

Plate 15. The Callanish Stones on the island of Lewis in the Hebrides.

PHOTOGRAPH BY THE AUTHOR

Plate 16. Leigh McCloskey's inner sanctum, dubbed The Hieroglyph of the Human Soul.

PHOTOGRAPH BY THE AUTHOR

15

A Garden of the Mysteries

The dots to be joined multiply as the years pass—books written and published, projects, conferences, journeys, friendships, chance encounters, family events, dramas, and celebrations in the lives of loved ones. Each is like a speck of microfilm that can be magnified to tell a whole story. As I cannot magnify each one I must be selective.

The year 2016 was a pivotal one, both internationally and domestically. It was the year of the Brexit referendum, which led to Britain deciding to cut loose from the European Union. It was also the year in which we moved house. Our terrace house in Bremen had been our home for twelve years, but Donate could no longer cope with its four stories, so we moved to a two-story house in Lilienthal, just outside Bremen. Here we once again set about creating a garden, but now we had an entirely different space to work with: at the front a rectangular garden with a lawn surrounded by bushes, and on the other three sides a strip of ground mostly consisting of shrubbery. There was also a paved terrace, pleasantly enclosed by the house, brick walls, and mature bushes.

Here we set out to create a Garden of the Mysteries, that is to say: (a) the classical mysteries of ancient Greece and Rome, (b) the

Fig. 15.1. Our front garden with sundial.
PHOTOGRAPH BY THE AUTHOR

Hermetic mysteries, and (c) the Germanic and Celtic mysteries of the north. Regretfully we left behind the obelisk in our old garden, but we took with us the sundial with the symbols of the elements and the compass directions. This will one day be our gravestone, symbolizing the endurance of love beyond mortality. Over the years we went on to add many more features, bearing in mind Ian Hamilton Finlay's concept of "a series of little points that go *zing!*"

The layout of the garden, running in a strip around the house, suggested the idea of creating an itinerary, a kind of mythical and magical pilgrimage, leading one through a succession of images that would evoke various aspects of the mysteries, but the difficulty was to find suitable features. Of course, in a garden center or builder's shop one can find an abundance of concrete cherubs, reproductions of the Venus de Milo, Buddhas, Japanese lanterns, and garden gnomes galore. Admittedly one can occasionally find something attractive in such places. For example, we have a concrete urn filled with shells—mostly gathered by Donate's granddaughters on the shores of Langeoog—which looks stunning against the dark foliage of some rhododendron bushes—but on the whole the mass-produced ornaments sold in garden centers are liable to look cheap and unattractive. And genuine stone garden sculptures are usually prohibitively expensive. So, faced with this situation, I decided to do something I had long been contemplating, namely to take up stone and wood carving myself.

Here I was inspired by Rudolf Steiner's view that spiritual wisdom should not be confined to the head or heart but should flow through our manual capacities into the material world. He, himself, practiced what he preached by applying his energies in many areas including art, architecture, education, dance, agriculture, and medicine. His visionary sculptures are extraordinarily powerful. I was also inspired by the example of the operative stonemasons' guilds, from which speculative Freemasonry emerged. The latter is often presented as somehow more elevated and more spiritual than the former, whereas I see, for example, the masons who built the Parthenon or Chartres Cathedral as having been highly spiritual men, who imbued their creations with a special kind of energy that one can still feel today. So, having been a man of the pen for most of my life, I now also took up the hammer and chisel.

One of the first things I created was an oracle in the form of a circle of flat, irregularly shaped slabs of natural stone incised with the twenty-four runes of the older runic alphabet (or Elder *Futhark*, to use the Norse word), which, like the Hebrew letters, represent forces and principles that operate in ourselves and in the world. I placed the stones in a half-hidden space in the shrubbery, surrounded by

Fig. 15.2. The Runic Circle in our garden in Lilienthal. It is
dedicated to the Norns, the three Nordic goddesses of time and
fate. See also color plate 11.

PHOTOGRAPH BY THE AUTHOR

rhododendron bushes, and beside it I placed a stone bench inscribed
with a dedication to the Norns, the three goddesses of time and fate:
Urd, Verdandi, and Skuld. I found that the ideal time to get a reading from the oracle is on sunny days with some clouds and a bit of
wind. Under these conditions light, filtered through the foliage and
falling on the stones, is continually shifting with the changing patterns of the clouds and the movement of the leaves in the wind, high-
lighting particular runes. In addition, leaves or blossoms will fall on
this or that rune, and sometimes an insect will crawl across a stone.
Occasionally, even a robin who seems fond of that spot will land on
a particular rune. In this way the stones are continually interacting
with nature to spell out a message.

Skeptics might dismiss all of this as fanciful nonsense, but not if they were aware of what has been called the field-based approach in science, popularized by the British scientist Rupert Sheldrake but pioneered earlier in the twentieth century by researchers such as the Russian Alexander Gurwitsch and the German Jewish émigré to England Herbert Fröhlich. These scientists have recognized that objects in the physical world, animate and inanimate, have energy fields that interact with each other. These fields are perceptible to the deeper levels of the human mind, which are thus connected to a network of fields that embraces the entire universe and arguably can transcend time. To access those deeper levels it is necessary to bypass the rational part of the mind, which can be done by means of images, symbols, and symbolically charged actions. This is essentially how divination methods such as dowsing, the I Ching, or the runes work.

Close to the oracle, against an ivy-covered wall and within sight of the bench, I placed a stele with a relief of Odin's two ravens, Hugin and Munin, representing thought and memory. Below the ravens I carved a poem in German, of which the English translation reads: "Hugin, raven of thought, Munin, raven of memory, fly high and far, come safely back." Thus I can sit opposite the stele, letting thought and memory roam or contemplating the stones, as the mood takes me.

For the Hermetic mysteries we had the sundial with the symbols of the compass directions and elements, which found a perfect place on our front lawn within a circle of box bushes, and I carved a stele with an ouroboros, the ancient alchemical symbol of a serpent biting its tail. The Celtic mysteries were represented by the head of a Green Man, which, as I mentioned, I had bought from a dealer in England. For the classical mysteries I made a stele to Pan, inscribed with the words "PAUSE AND LISTEN TO PAN'S ARCADIAN PIPES"—inviting one to hear Pan's music in the form of the birdsong and the sound of the wind in the trees. This was placed against

Fig. 15.3. A stele to the god Pan on our terrace in Lilienthal. See also color plate 12.

PHOTOGRAPH BY THE AUTHOR

Fig. 15.4. Prayer beads placed on the terrace by Donate. See also color plate 13.

PHOTOGRAPH BY DONATE MCINTOSH

an ivy-covered wall on one side of the terrace. Also on the terrace Donate placed strings of shells and colorful prayer beads.

Also in the classical tradition, we had inherited, along with the house, a relief of a graceful maenad in a semi-diaphanous garment, which fitted neatly into a niche in the wall at the back of the terrace. To fill a smaller niche in the same wall I made a clay relief of a head of Apollo with the inscription "To the Apollo of the north." This pair reflects Friedrich Nietzsche's dichotomy between the Apollonian and Dionysiac modes—Apollo embodying light, beauty, and order, and Dionysus—in this case represented by a maenad—embodying passion, intoxication, and frenzy. The ancient Greeks, through their dramas, found a way to reconcile these two modalities, something that we in the modern West are perpetually struggling with.

Around each of the niches I painted a trompe l'oeil frame in classical style, which gave a whole new vitality to the reliefs. In designing and painting these frames—their proportions, decorative motifs, and colors—I had the feeling that I was being guided by the spirit of the classical tradition. I remembered Ian Hamilton Finlay describing something very similar that he experienced at Little Sparta when he began to place works of art in the landscape. Whenever he felt in doubt about how to place a work he would put himself in touch with the classical tradition and invariably receive guidance.

Another feature I made that was taken from classical mythology was an owl, sacred to the goddess Athene, carved out of a log and painted in different colors and placed near the front door, with an inscription in German inviting the visitor to "look around with the open eyes of the owl and the wisdom of the goddess." When I was preparing to make this figure an extraordinary coincidence occurred. I was sitting at a table with a computer in front of me, looking for a picture of an owl that I could use as a model for the sculpture. Donate was watching a quiz show on television close by, and I heard the quizmaster asking a female contestant what her favorite animal

Fig. 15.5. Plaster relief of a maenad, surrounded by
a trompe l'oeil frame. See also color plate 14.
PHOTOGRAPH BY THE AUTHOR

was. In the instant that a picture of an owl appeared on my computer screen I heard the woman reply: "An owl." The universe thinking aloud again! Some say that is the first sign of madness, so was the universe going slightly mad, or was the goddess Athene teasing me, or was it that at that moment the deeper levels of my mind were open to that invisible, all-encompassing network? Perhaps it was all three. At any rate, I have found that when we activate those deeper levels of ourselves such coincidences start to happen.

Fig. 15.6. Making a clay model of the Irminsul, sacred pillar of the Saxons, in an atelier at the Robinson holiday club in 2019.

PHOTOGRAPH FROM THE AUTHOR'S COLLECTION

My woodcarving tools also serve for making ceremonial objects, such as the staff that I made from a fallen branch found in a wood. To the top end of the staff I fitted a piece of wood carved into a shape like two outward-reaching bows curled at the ends—a design based on the Irminsul, the sacred pillar of the Saxons, destroyed by Charlemagne in 772 during his Christianization campaign.

Another representation of the Irminsul, which I made in clay and fired in a kiln at a high temperature, I find to be a good object for meditation, either held in the hand or placed on a table. I also made a set of runestaves in beechwood with the letters engraved using a soldering iron.

I have found that the making of such objects becomes in itself a meditation like the work of the alchemists. If the work is carried out in a mood of inner stillness, reverence, and concentration, something of that mood is transferred to the things that one creates. They in turn will give off positive energy to other people.

16

In Search of the Northern Gods

Meanwhile, in August 2016 it was back to the enchanted land of Iceland for a New York Open Center Esoteric Quest on the Mysteries of the North—my third visit to the country at intervals of about twenty years, the previous one having been in 2003 for Hilmar's installation as Allsherjargoði, head of the Icelandic Asatru movement. I was curious to see how the country had developed in the meantime and in particular how the Asatru community was faring.

Hilmar met me at the airport and drove me to his house on the Álftanes peninsula just outside Reykjavik, where he lived with his wife, Ragna, an artist and novelist, and his two teenage daughters, Sólveig and Erna Maria. The following day he took me to the site where a new Asatru temple, designed by the architect Magnús Jensson, was being constructed in a hilly area to the southeast of the city to cater to the rapidly growing number of Asatru followers. The site was against a cliff, part of which had been blasted away to make room for the foundation. A bulldozer was at work, and channels had been dug for cables and pipes. At the edge of the site a stone monument had been erected to Sveibjörn Benteinnsen, the farmer and poet who had founded the Asatru movement in the 1970s. Today at the time of writing the temple is only partly built, owing to a shortage of funds and problems in obtaining materials, but a section containing administrative offices is occupied and functioning. This is the first pagan temple for many centuries to be built in Europe. Others are now springing up in various countries.

The next afternoon I had an impulse to call Ralph White on my mobile phone, as I suddenly thought: Was it today that I was supposed to be joining the conference group for a bus journey to the venue? Somehow I had become confused about the date. Sure enough, the bus was due to leave at 2:30 and it was already 2:10. Ralph said it would be all right if I got there by 3:00, which I just managed after Hilmar drove me to Álftanes to collect my suitcase and then back into Reykjavik. Boarding the bus I was greeted by many speakers and guests from previous Esoteric Quests. After an overnight stop at Selfoss, we drove on in a northwesterly direction to the Hotel Hellnar at Bogarnes on the Snaefels peninsula, which was our main venue. It was close to a coastline of jagged, volcanic cliffs and overlooked by a bare, rather forbidding mountain sacred to the god Barður, one of the personae of Odin. A description of him in one of the sagas corresponds closely to J. R. R. Tolkien's description of the wizard Gandalf in *Lord of the Rings*. What better place to hold a conference on the mysteries of the north?

The first plenary lecture was by Leonard George, a Canadian psychologist and friend from previous Quests, who spoke about the ways in which the mystique of the north has been carried down over the centuries. He talked about the voyage in the fourth century BCE of the Greek mariner Pytheas, who sailed from Marseilles out into the Atlantic and northward to a land of mist and fog, which he called Thule and which may have been Iceland. The lecture also touched on many other themes: the pole star; the invisible forces that are said to flow northward; Johann Kepler's notion of Iceland as being the place nearest to the moon; Jules Verne's story *Journey to the Center of the Earth* via Iceland; and the concept of the Buddha of the North, one of the five Dhyani Buddhas corresponding to the four compass points and the center.

This lecture set the tone for a rich program covering many aspects of the northern mysteries including a fascinating talk by another friend and veteran Quester, Scott Olsen from Florida, who spoke about a half-hidden northern tradition involving the use of narcotic substances as indicated in certain symbols such as the hammer of Thor, which Scott believed to represent a psychedelic mushroom. I myself gave a talk on "The Legacy of Nordic and Teutonic Mythology," and Hilmar came for part of the conference to speak about Asatru and to play a recording of a musical work called *Odin's Raven Magic*, performed by the legendary Icelandic rock band Sigur Rós, with which Hilmar had been involved as a musician and composer.

On the bus back to Reykjavik after the end of the conference I was sitting next to Scott Olsen, who suggested that I turn the substance of my talk into a book. Accordingly, after returning home I wrote a book synopsis and, after a false start with one publisher, submitted it to Weiser Books, who enthusiastically accepted the proposal. In due course the book was published under the title *Beyond the North Wind*.

Soon after I returned from Iceland Donate and I went to Berlin for an event called the Long Night of the Religions, a kind of interfaith festival in which many different religions presented themselves at various venues throughout the city. The Pagans took over a kind of family community center in the eastern part of Berlin. There were stalls for Asatru, Wicca, Reclaiming, the Druids, and other groups, and there was a program of lectures, including one by Donate on Goddess worship. The festival culminated in a multifaith gathering at the Gendarmenmarkt in the city center. The media were there in force, but typically they paid very little attention to the Pagans.

In November I went to Prague where I made contact with Lionel and Lynn, who were visiting Europe and had decided to spend a few days in the Czech capital along with their friends David and Susan Gilbert from England. One of the highlights of our visit was a guided tour of the alchemy museum, Speculum Alchemiae, featuring a well-preserved alchemical laboratory that had been created on the initiative of Rudolf II, Holy Roman Emperor from 1576 to 1612. Because alchemy was frowned upon by the church, the laboratory was highly secret. It was hidden in the cellar of a building in the Jewish quarter that was ostensibly an apothecary's shop. The emperor had gone there by way of a secret tunnel running beneath the river Moldau to the royal palace on the opposite side. During a flood in 2002 the laboratory was exposed, complete with furnaces, flasks, distilling equipment, and a book containing alchemical recipes.

Our guided tour was like something out of a Harry Potter film. In a back room in the former apothecary's shop the guide pushed aside one section of a bookcase to reveal a stone spiral staircase leading down to the cellar containing the remains of three chambers, one for plant alchemy, another for work involving metals, and a third where glassblowers made the alchemical vessels. Being in that underground laboratory took me into the Rosicrucian world that I had written so much about. I could almost smell the fumes and hear the footsteps of the emperor Rudolf approaching down his secret passage, perhaps accompanied by the English magus John Dee and his friend the alchemist Edward Kelley.

During the Prague visit I also made contact with Vladislav Zadrobilek's daughter Zuzana, who had taken over her father's shop and publishing business, but was operating from a new address. I took Lionel to meet her and we had a pleasant chat in a nearby café with a couple of young men who were friends of hers.

A particularly memorable event—memorable in a rather curious way—was the winter solstice ritual for 2016, which I celebrated in the Asatru manner with friends at a venue that was new to me, located in the country near Wilhelmshaven. There were about seven of us, including the *godi* (person leading the ceremony), who was a much-respected figure in the Asatru community. It was late in the afternoon by the time we sat down to talk through the program, and the godi, with a glass of beer in front of him, spoke at inordinate length about every aspect of the ritual and insisted that every song be rehearsed in full, while we grew increasingly impatient. Darkness fell, and finally we went outside into the backyard of the house while each of us was brushed by smoke from a censer containing an herbal preparation. When it was the godi's turn we could see that he had drunk too much, as he was swaying and staggering.

We proceeded to the back of the garden, where an altar had been set up. While the godi looked on, a fire was lit, a horn was sounded, and a hammer of Thor was raised at the four quarters to consecrate and shield the space. Now it was time for the godi to step forward and lead the main proceedings, but it was clear that he was in no fit state to do so, as it was all he could do to stand up straight. Someone asked me if I could take over and lead the ritual, which I did. I suggested that we ask the gods to send their strength to the godi. Another participant leapt to my support and got us to join hands and all together send positive energy to the godi. The ritual went on and it came to the part where a mead horn was circulated. At the third round I proposed that we drink to the godi. I spoke of all he had done for our religion and how it was thanks to him that we were celebrating together on that night. I said that we were not just a ritual circle but a group who supported each other. The person standing beside me put his arm around me and said some heartfelt words of affirmation. We sang the final song, "O Tannenbaum," and joined hands to make a "wishing bridge"—a way of sending our wishes into the world. The godi managed to speak a few words. We raised our hands outward and upward to send our wishes on their way, and the ritual was concluded. The ways of the gods can be unexpected. What at one point had seemed like a catastrophe had turned into one of the most moving rituals I have ever experienced and created a deep bond between all of those present.

17

Civis Germanicus

By the beginning of 2017 I had been living in Germany for nearly twenty-four years, and I decided to apply for German citizenship. This was partly prompted by the impending exit of Britain from the European Union (the so-called Brexit), which I thought might create problems for me if I merely had a German residence permit, but mainly the decision was out of solidarity with my adopted country and the country of my wife. At our local folk high school, along with thirteen other applicants from various countries, I took a general knowledge test about Germany involving basic questions about the constitution, the legal system, voting rights, the system of government at the federal and regional level, and so on. I also had to submit a variety of personal documents to the regional government office in the town of Osterholz. Then I was told that I would have to wait several months for the formal naturalization. Around the same time my son Angus, who by then was living in Hamburg with his partner, Katja, also successfully applied to become a German citizen.

In the meantime I had a full program of trips, conferences, and other activities. One seminal event for me that year was the sixth conference of the European Society for the Study of

Esotericism (ESSWE), which was held in June in the beautiful town of Erfurt. The conference venue was a former Augustinian monastery where Martin Luther had been a novice, and which was now a Lutheran conference center and hotel. There were many old friends present, and I made two new ones who were to play an important role in my life. One was Aaron French, a young scholar from California who was working on a PhD dissertation about Max Weber and Rudolf Steiner. In conversation with him during a break in the program we discovered that we were both Freemasons, and Aaron raised the idea of my giving a lecture at his lodge in Oakland. This meeting subsequently led to a whole new chapter in my life.

The other important contact I made in Erfurt was with Zhenya Gershman, a Russian Jewish artist who had emigrated to the United States and married an American scientist. She was now living in Los Angeles where she had a studio and ran an organization called Aesthetics of Western Esotericism (AWE). I was deeply impressed by a lecture she gave in Erfurt on Albrecht Dürer's famous engraving known under the title of *Melencolia*. Zhenya convincingly demolished the usual interpretations of the engraving and revealed it to be packed with esoteric symbolism. She subsequently made me a fellow of AWE, and we developed a fruitful cooperation.

A couple of months after Erfurt came another Esoteric Quest organized by the New York Open Center, this time at Stornoway on the island of Lewis in the Hebrides. I flew first to Edinburgh where I stayed for a night with my stepmother, Karina, and together with my niece Lucy we visited Little Sparta, a rather weird experience, as the place is now in the hands of a trust and is open to the public. You can no longer drive up the dirt road to the house but have to park at the foot of the drive and walk up the hill. The house itself has become a museum with an entry charge, a bookstall, and a study room. I remembered how the place was when Ian was still alive and how we would sit in the cozy, book-crammed living room talking over endless cups of strong tea. It made me feel slightly melancholy, but I cheered up when we walked around the garden and I saw how it had retained its magic and how beautifully it was being maintained, obviously attracting many visitors. Later I sent the bookstall some copies of my Finlay memoir.

Next day I flew on to Stornoway. The conference venue was Lews Castle, a great Victorian gothic pile, built by James Mathieson, who had made a fortune shipping opium into India from China. Now a hotel, it stood on a hill overlooking the town and harbor. One of the first items on the program was a bus trip to Ness in the north of the island to visit a community of the Free Church (colloquially known as the Wee Frees). On the way our local guide Alistair McIntosh (no relation) explained their austere Calvinist doctrine, which involved the notion of "unconditional election," meaning that certain people are chosen by God to go to heaven, regardless of their piety or merit. The rest are condemned to go to hell no matter what. One might think that such a grim religion would produce a grim type of mentality, but the members of the Free Church community in Ness were warm, friendly, and welcoming. We were served refreshments at an information center and museum, and then were taken to a church hall to hear a performance of psalm singing in Gaelic. It remains for me a paradox that the delightful people we met should adhere to such a gloomy creed.

On another expedition we were taken to the Callanish Stones, a complex of megalithic circles erected some five thousand years ago and thus predating Stonehenge. The stones are believed to be geared to a lunar cycle of 18.6 years. Once in every cycle the moon appears to skim over a range of hills on the horizon, which resemble a recumbent woman. This was my first visit to the site, and I was struck, as I had been at Stonehenge and Avebury, by the thought of an advanced culture having existed in these northern latitudes long before even the Egyptian pyramids were built, belying the narrative that civilization

Fig. 17.1. The Callanish Stones on the island of Lewis in the Hebrides. See also color plate 15.

PHOTOGRAPH BY THE AUTHOR

originally spread from south to north. Further evidence of this came in a lecture by Nicholas Cope, a British expert on sacred geometry, who spoke about a prehistoric site in the Orkney Islands called the Knap of Howar. Consisting of two stone-walled chambers side by side, connected by a passage, the site reveals a knowledge of certain key proportions and measurements, such as the golden section and the megalithic yard, postulated by Alexander Thom in the 1950s.

Other presentations at the conferences included one on the runes by Halvard Harklau, and talks by myself on Freemasonry in Scotland and on Ian Hamilton Finlay and Little Sparta. On one evening there was also a *ceilidh* with much Scottish country dancing.

Soon after returning home I was formally made a German citizen in the regional government office in Osterholz, where I arrived in the early afternoon with Donate and my close friend Jörg Rohfeld. The proceedings took place in the chamber of the regional assembly, where there were ten other people being naturalized, plus their friends and relatives. The new citizens included some young Arab men, a woman from Brazil, and three British women. The ceremony was led by Bernd Lütjen, a member of the assembly, assisted by Frau Ewe, who had processed my application. There were also two other men and another woman from the administration.

Herr Lütjen conducted the ceremony with a nice mixture of lightness and dignity. Each new citizen was invited to come forward and say a few words about their reasons for wanting German citizenship. They then received a certificate of naturalization and a copy of the German constitution and shook hands with Herr Lütjen and the two women officials. The three British women all gave Brexit as their reason for seeking citizenship. When it was my turn I said that for me Brexit had been the trigger but not the main reason. Having lived for twenty-three years in Germany and being married to a German woman, I felt good in Germany and in Lilienthal and now wanted to take a more active part in German communal life. I also mentioned that the previous Friday had been my seventy-fourth birthday and that the naturalization was a nice birthday present. After the ceremony a photograph was taken of the group, and coffee and biscuits were served.

On the drive back home through lovely countryside in the mellow autumn sunshine I felt quite lightheaded. I had sealed a bond with my adopted country, while keeping my British citizenship as well, and now I had the sense that yet another phase in my life was beginning.

18

California Ho!

In the spring of 2018 I went on an exciting lecture trip to California. Disembarking from the plane at San Francisco airport, I remembered my great-grandfather Thomas Wheeler going there in the gold rush and all the adventures he had been through—the brothel masquerading as a shirt factory, the murder of his gold-prospecting partner, his abortive raid on the jail, and the bag of gold dust that he had taken back east.

My visit was rather less fraught. My friend Aaron, whom I had met in Erfurt, had put me in touch with his Masonic lodge Templum Rosae in Oakland, which later accepted me as an honorary member and then as a full member. I was scheduled to speak there and at the Oakland Scottish Rite. Jonathan Prestage, a leading member of both bodies, met me at the airport and drove me to my hotel in Oakland. Over the next couple of days I lectured to the Scottish Rite on the links between Freemasonry and Rosicrucianism, and to Templum Rosae on the Hermetic Order of the Golden Dawn and the Fräulein Sprengel correspondence. I also went with a group of Brethren down to San Jose to visit Rosicrucian Park, the premises of the Ancient Mystical Order Rosae Crucis (AMORC), which included an Egyptian museum, a permanent exhibition on alchemy, and the tomb of the founder Harvey Spence Lewis in the form of a pyramid. Lewis was undoubtedly a genius of sorts, and AMORC was and is one of the most interesting offshoots of the Rosicrucian tree.

I then flew down to Los Angeles and went up the coast to Malibu to stay with my friends Leigh and Carla McCloskey and give a lecture to a group of their friends and neighbors in the form of a preview of my forthcoming book on the mystique of the north. Leigh and Carla both previously had careers in the film industry—Leigh as an actor and Carla as a director. Leigh studied acting at the Juilliard School in New York, where his fellow student and roommate was the actor Robin Williams. After a long and highly successful career with prominent roles in television series such as *Dallas, California Clan,* and *General Hospital,* he achieved equal success as a visionary artist of genius. The McCloskeys' house, in a beautiful area uphill from the coast and set in a lovely garden, is itself a work of art, especially the inner sanctum on the upper floor, which Leigh has named The Hieroglyph of the Human Soul. The room is an Aladdin's Cave, in which you are enveloped by his astonishing paintings, which extend over the walls, the floor, and even over the backs of the books on the shelves. Also visiting the house when I arrived was the writer and alchemist Stanislas ("Stash") Klossowski de Rola, son of the famous painter Balthus.

After three nights in Malibu I took a bus down to Santa Monica and made my way to the Santa Monica Masonic Center where I was given a guest room. The same evening I gave a talk to an audience of about 150 people under the title "The Rose Cross and the Square and Compass." The following day I visited the house of Zhenya Gershman and her husband and daughter, and saw her studio. I learned that her grandfather Mikhail Matusovsky wrote the words of the song "Midnight in Moscow," which I remembered being a big international hit back in the 1960s.

Fig. 18.1. The writer and alchemist Stanislas Klossowski de Rola (*left*) and the artist Leigh McCloskey in the garden of the McCloskeys' house at Malibu, California, in 2018.

PHOTOGRAPH BY THE AUTHOR

Fig. 18.2. Leigh's inner sanctum, dubbed The Hieroglyph of the Human Soul. See also color plate 16.

PHOTOGRAPH BY THE AUTHOR

Another encounter during that visit was with a young actor, singer, performance artist, and filmmaker calling himself Amen Ra, who had read my book on King Ludwig II of Bavaria and wanted to collaborate with me in making a film about him. I later learned that his real name was Jakub Stepniak and that he had also used the pseudonym Kuba Ka. He had been born in 1986 at Gdansk in Poland, where his father was a professor of economics, and as a child he had been a famous singing star in Poland. When I met him for lunch at the Casa del Mar hotel in Santa Monica he presented a startling appearance: expensive looking black leather outfit, calf-length boots, ankh pendant, sunglasses, jet-black hair that had evidently been dyed, and a handsome face that looked as though he had applied some kind of artificial tan. He proved to be extremely friendly, charming, and charismatic with a certain childlike quality, and was bubbling over

Fig. 18.3. Myself with the actor and singer Jakub Stepniak
(alias Amen Ra, alias Kuba Ka) having lunch at the
Casa del Mar hotel in Santa Monica, California, in 2018.

PHOTOGRAPH FROM THE AUTHOR'S COLLECTION

with enthusiasm about the prospect of making a film about Ludwig. I told him I would be happy to help him in any way I could.

While I was in LA my Masonic brother Daniel Rivera, who had arranged the Santa Monica lecture assignment, took me to the Theosophical center in the Hollywood district, where we heard a lecture on the subject of synchronicity by Stephan Hoeller, the renowned expert on Gnosticism and founder of the Ecclesia Gnostica. Afterward I had a chat with Hoeller, a Hungarian by origin, who told me how he had come to Gnosticism. At the age of three he dreamt of a huge devil figure holding the world in his claws and squeezing it so hard that moisture dripped from it. At the age of 11 he began to read about Gnosticism and made a connection with the dream. He went on to write many books about Gnosticism and Jungian psychology and to become active in the neo-Gnostic movement.

The following day I had breakfast with Daniel at a café on Santa Monica Boulevard, and then he drove me to the airport for my flight home. Two months later the news came of terrible forest fires in California, especially in the north. With bated breath I followed on the internet the course of the fire in the Malibu area and saw that the street on which the McCloskeys lived appeared to be directly in its path. Later I heard Leigh's account of the drama that they went through. As the inferno drew closer the police ordered all the residents in the area to leave. The McCloskeys ignored the order and stayed to fight the fire, which they perceived as a raging beast, consumed by pure anger. While sparks from the burning buildings across the street rained down on their home, they struggled night and day to protect it, hosing down the sparks and spreading wet blankets on the roof of the house. At last the fires subsided, leaving a scene of devastation, but their home had been spared.

A year later, in May 2019, I returned to California. In the meantime my book *Beyond the North Wind* had been published, and the Oakland Scottish Rite put on a launch event combined with a talk by me to introduce the book. I also gave a lecture to Templum Rosae Lodge on "Scotland and the Craft." I then flew down to Los Angeles to stay with my niece Pollyanna McIntosh, a highly successful actress and film director. She has featured in cult TV series such as *The Walking Dead* and *Vikings: Valhalla*, and has starred in films like *The Woman* and its sequel *Darlin'*, which she also wrote and directed. She went with me to the Philosophical Research Society, where I was welcomed by the director, Greg Salyer, and the librarian and program organizer Kelly Carmena, who had arranged a launch-cum-lecture event for me in connection with *Beyond the North Wind*. Also present were Zhenya Gershman, who introduced my talk, Leigh McCloskey, Stash de Rola, and Amen Ra.

The following evening Amen invited me to dinner at the Tam O'Shanter restaurant, the favorite haunt of Walt Disney, whose regular table was marked with a brass plaque. Amen was wearing an extraordinary pair of shoes, covered in spikes as though made from two hedgehog skins and all painted in gold. We discussed the project for the Ludwig film and the possibility of basing the screenplay partly on my story *The Cult of Uvik*. Amen of course would be the obvious choice to play the role of the king.

The next day I went by bus up to Malibu to visit Leigh and Carla. Leigh drove me around the area and showed me the devastation from the fires a year earlier. About 170 houses in their neighborhood had been destroyed, and the remains had been completely cleared away, leaving only empty lots, charred trees, and scorched bits of ground. A few houses and quite a lot of vegetation had escaped the fire, and already new growth was springing up here and there. I took an Uber back to Polly's house in LA, and the following day she took me to visit the Hollyhock House, designed by Frank Lloyd Wright—a much overestimated architect in my opinion. The house had an arresting design, but after it was finished the roof leaked, and there were crazy features like a water channel running through the living room, inviting someone to trip into it. After one more night at Polly's house I flew back to Germany.

After returning home I continued to correspond with Amen Ra by email about the Ludwig project and had several telephone calls with his father Andrzej Stepniak, who was also involved in the planning but died unexpectedly in December 2019. In addition I arranged an internship in Amen's studio for Eva, the daughter of our friend Corinna Reynolds. Eva was thrilled with Los Angeles and charmed by Amen, who was prepared to give her a long-term job in the studio when she finished her studies. Meanwhile Amen had been scouting out locations for the Ludwig film and said he would invite me out to LA and put me up in a top hotel so that we could take the film project a stage further. Our correspondence continued into 2021. Then in April of that year Amen suddenly died at the age of thirty-five from a mysterious affliction that caused terrible skin lesions and may have been due to an infection that he had picked up in Africa some years earlier. They say that those whom the gods love die young, and indeed the gods had showered him with abundant gifts. In his short life he'd had a remarkable career. He possessed a kind of childlike innocence and charm, which endeared him to many. I feel glad to have known him, for however short a time. May he rest in peace.

19

The Gods Give and the Gods Take Away

After the appearance of *Beyond the North Wind* I began to receive invitations to give interviews on various podcast channels. I also took part in a launch at the Atlantis Bookshop in London in July 2019. The Atlantis team hosted the event beautifully and displayed copies of the book in the window. About twenty-five or thirty people were there, including Joscelyn Godwin, who was visiting London at the time, my sons Angus and Jason, my brother David, my old college friend Barney Powell, and some whom I had not seen for years, like the pagan folk singer Ian Read and some former MA students from the Exeter esotericism program. Afterward a group of us repaired for dinner to a Greek restaurant nearby.

A few months later I found myself in London again for another meeting of the Anonymous Society, this time at Barney Powell's club, the Naval and Military, in St. James's Square. On the way there I took the underground to Green Park, and as I stepped out on to the platform a foreign-looking man came toward me with a big smile and exclaimed: "Doctor! Doctor!" Taken aback, I wondered whether I had perhaps met him in some academic context but no longer remembered him. I said: "Yes, I'm Dr. McIntosh," to which he replied: "Oh, thank you so much for operating on me!" Such incidents of mistaken identity used to happen to me quite frequently, but I had never before been taken for a surgeon! In this case the mistake was soon cleared up and the man, who turned out to be from Iran, went on his way, while I went on to our writers' meeting.

By then I was looking for a topic for a new book and was thinking about writing something on Russia. In *Beyond the North Wind* I had devoted two chapters to the mystique of the north in Russia and had become aware of the great spiritual resurgence that was taking place there in the wake of the collapse of communism. I had also made contact with a number of people from the Russian intellectual and cultural milieu such as the artist Alexander Uglanov, creator of striking visionary images of Hyperborea and of pagan Russia. A book on Russia from the spiritual and esoteric point of view seemed like an obvious idea for the next project. I submitted a proposal to Inner Traditions, which was accepted, and I started work on the book, which appeared in due course under the title *Occult Russia*.

This was 2020, the year when Brexit finally happened and the Covid epidemic started, with all the attendant restrictions, lockdowns, and crisis measures. The first consequence of Covid for me was that I had to cancel a trip to the United States that I had planned for May. The University of California at Davis was going to host a conference of the Association for the Study of Esotericism on the theme of "Esotericism and the Scientific Imagination" under the coordination of Allison Coudert, professor of religious studies. I had agreed to give a keynote speech surveying half a century of the study of esotericism, and I was going to combine the assignment with lecture trips to Oakland and Los Angeles. At the Philosophical Research Society in LA I was going to give a talk on King Ludwig II as a teaser for the film about him that I was planning with Amen Ra. I had even sketched out a publicity flyer announcing: "A king in search of the Holy Grail—the enchanted world of Ludwig II of Bavaria . . . and introducing the forthcoming motion picture *The Swan King*, a creation of Amen Ra studios, featuring Amen Ra in the role of King Ludwig." Amen himself was going to be present at the talk, and I had the idea that he could appear disguised as the king.

By early 2020 it was clear that the conference in Davis would have to be canceled or postponed on account of Covid, and Allison sent out a notice to that effect. This meant that I would also have to cancel the rest of my trip. I had already booked my travel, but fortunately there was a freeze on flights to the US at the time in question, so I was able to get a refund from the travel agent.

In July 2020 came another death out of the blue, that of my old friend Jörg Rohfeld. On a Monday his daughter Julia telephoned me to tell me the news that he had died in his bed the week before and been found by his mother in the morning. I was stunned. He had suffered a serious stroke a year or so earlier, but appeared to be recovering well and had begun to take part in rituals again. Only a month earlier I had celebrated midsummer with him and a couple of other friends. Julia told me that an urn burial was to take place the following Saturday in the cemetery of the church in his village, Oppeln, and she felt that I would be the best person to lead the memorial ceremony. I telephoned various of our Asatru friends and hurriedly put together a program and prepared a speech.

In fine summer weather I drove over to Oppeln. The little church was situated down a lane in an idyllic, leafy setting. Beside the graveyard was a small building for memorial ceremonies, which had been beautifully arranged by the undertakers, with candles, flowers, and photographs of Jörg. I gave an address in which I surveyed Jörg's many-faceted life and the experiences we had shared. His son-in-law Daniel played a recording of a folk song performed by Jörg's choir in the 1980s, and there were addresses by Daniel and by members of our Asatru association. After the ceremony we went out into the graveyard for the urn burial. A member of Jörg's rifle-shooting club said some words and laid a wreath, then a group from his hunting club blew a salute on their hunting horns. The mourners strewed petals and other offerings into the grave. I offered petals, a twig of the sacred yew tree, and a small pendant from Donate with a Celtic pattern. Goodbye, old friend. *Bit 'n anner mol,* as they say in Low German when they mean "I'll be seeing you."

Meanwhile the Covid epidemic and the lockdown continued. It became clear that many of the effects would be permanent. The new year 2021 arrived and a mass vaccination program was started. Everywhere businesses were closing, including our favorite spa and wellness center, the Oase in Bremen. Another result of the lockdown was that more and more conferences were being conducted online. The New York Open Center held its first online Esoteric Quest in October 2020, and I spoke on the classical art of memory. Since then online conferences have become familiar events.

The spring of 2021 brought another bereavement with the death of Ingrid. It was the end of an era for me. Ever since the time when she was a lodger at our house in Edinburgh in the 1950s she had been—with some intervals—part of my life for nearly seventy years as a kind of wise aunt or fairy godmother. She represented the old Germany from before the war, the country of poets, thinkers, and high culture, and her house had always been for me a part of that Germany. A final farewell to her came in August when relatives held an urn burial at sea, as Ingrid had wanted. I traveled to the harbor of Niendorf on the Baltic coast where I joined up with a party of relatives and friends of Ingrid and we boarded a motor yacht run by a firm specializing in sea burials. In glorious, sunny weather we sailed out into Lübeck Bay while the ship's captain gave a memorial address. Then we went out on to the rear deck and a member of the crew lowered the urn, topped with a bouquet of flowers, into the sea. A basket with more flowers was passed around, and we threw them into the water in the direction of the urn. While the vessel circled the spot, we watched while the urn slowly sank and the bright petals tossed about on the glistening, sparkling waves.

A few days later Donate went into the local hospital for a replacement operation on her right hip, which went well. She then went for convalescence to the Bückeberg clinic at Bad Eilsen near Hannover, where I was able to visit her. Bad Eilsen is one of those old-fashioned spas that are scarce in England but still flourish in central Europe. It breathes the atmosphere that Thomas Mann describes in his novel *The Magic Mountain*. The elegant buildings of the spa complex surround a beautiful park where we strolled one evening along a small river, past rose beds and fountains making dancing, swirling patterns in the autumn sunlight. After three weeks in this idyllic place, and having received an intensive rehabilitation program, Donate was able to return home. Two months later we celebrated her seventieth birthday with a big tea party for family and friends in a local restaurant and a supper afterward at home. My brother, David, and my son Jason both came from England for the occasion. David and I got out our guitars and sang songs. Among the guests were friends that Donate had known for a very long time: Beate had been a friend for over sixty years since primary school, Birgitta for over fifty years since high school days, and Linda for over forty years. These and many others made it a heartwarming celebration.

20

The Rose Cross and the Internet

I once wrote a whimsical story called "The Meyerbeck Manuscript," set in the seventeenth century and involving the Rosicrucian brotherhood and the discovery of Christian Rosenkreuz's tomb, which was said to contain various wondrous objects including a *minutus mundus* or miniature world, a sort of universal compendium of all knowledge. I suggested flippantly that this object was in fact a computer connected to the internet. The narrator of the story is a young Rosicrucian brother who discovers the device and keeps it in his possession although he feels uneasy about it and is unable to decide whether it is an invention of God or of the devil. That was also my reaction when I first bought a computer and had access to the internet, and since then the negative and positive aspects of the digital world have both become obvious: on the one hand, the potential for fraud, libel, misinformation, propaganda, social control, and the corruption of minds through addiction to the artificial world of the computer screen; on the other hand, the vast, magical capabilities of digital technology, thanks to which I can design a website, make a film, create a virtual world, access a book or a lecture on virtually any subject, have a video conversation with a friend on the other side of the world, or attend a conference in virtual reality. The challenge is to use digital technology for our benefit while avoiding its abuses.

Consider, for example, the field of education. In many countries there is a general dumbing down taking place at all levels from primary school to university, and lecturers complain of students downloading their essays from the internet and being glued to their mobile phones during lectures. At the same time, digital technology can provide a marvelous facility for those genuinely hungry for knowledge and educational fare that is inspiring and uplifting.

Someone who shares my concern about these issues is my old friend Arthur Versluis, professor of religious studies at Michigan State University and author of numerous books on religion, philosophy, mysticism, literature, sacred geography, and more. In the academic year 2021–22 Arthur took a one-year sabbatical to research and write a book titled *American Gnosis* and, during this time, also develop an online educational platform called the Hieros Institute, whose purpose, as stated on its website, is "to develop our shared understanding of the sacred in both theory and practice." The site includes a series of podcast conversations with thinkers, writers, poets, artists, and scholars who share the essential vision of Hieros. Those podcasts that Arthur and I have made together include conversations with Frederick Turner on beauty, with Lionel Snell on re-enchantment, with Aaron French on occult fiction, with Leigh McCloskey on art and the spiritual, and with John Michael Greer on our vision for the future. The site also contains courses such as "Becoming Conscious," a journey of inner discovery, involving experiential exercises, and a course of my own entitled "Creating a Sacred Garden."

I finished writing *Occult Russia* in August 2021 and shortly afterward submitted a proposal for a book titled *Occult Germany*, which was also accepted by Inner Traditions. While I waited for

Occult Russia to be processed by the publisher, tensions were building up on the Russia-Ukraine frontier. In February 2022 Russian forces entered eastern Ukraine, and suddenly the nightmare of a major war in Europe became a reality. I began to wonder whether, in the circumstances, the publication of *Occult Russia* would be shelved, but it went ahead and the book came out at the end of 2022. Once again I received many requests for podcast interviews, and I was struck by the fact that none of my interviewers expressed any anti-Russian feeling. This was in contrast to the general mood of Russophobia purveyed by the mainstream media and most of the leading politicians, which I found distressing, as I had developed some warm personal contacts in Russia.

One person whom I had written about in the book and elsewhere was the influential philosopher and writer on geopolitics Alexander Dugin, who has been unfairly portrayed as a bogeyman in the West, although I doubt whether most of his critics have read a single word of what he has written. One does not have to agree with everything he says to appreciate the remarkable breadth and incisiveness of his mind. I was deeply shocked and outraged by the murder of his daughter Darya in August 2022 and felt that there should have been much stronger condemnation of it in the Western media. Dugin has said that in a civilized society it should be possible to engage in a dialogue with one's opponents, a principle famously upheld by Voltaire when he said that he might reject a person's opinion but would defend to the death their right to hold it. Increasingly this principle is being thrown overboard in the Western public arena.

As I write, I have the feeling that many of the pillars of the world that I grew up in are falling. One of them was Queen Elizabeth of Great Britain, who died on September 8, 2022, at the age of ninety-six. Since my early childhood she had been an unshakeable icon of the nation. I remembered her coronation, her jubilee, and the many crises that she had faced within her family. I even shook hands with her once when she visited the offices of the magazine where I was working. Having been an anti-monarchist for a short period as a teenager, I became a great supporter of the institution of monarchy. I watched the televised parades and ceremonies to bid her farewell and was struck by the huge display of public emotion, with people waiting all night to watch the funeral procession or to walk past the coffin in Westminster Abbey. I also watched the coronation of the new king, Charles III, and felt that he made a dignified impression. When I argue with people who say that monarchy is irrational and outdated I point out that a country has a soul, which does not respond to rational arguments but to symbols, traditions, and rituals—in a word, to magic.

The monarchist and the pagan make good bedfellows, as the concept of kingship goes far back into pagan times when the king was the ruler of a tribe or community rooted in a particular region rather than the ruler of a nation—the latter kind of monarchy came later with the growth of nation-states. The word *king* itself probably comes from the Anglo-Saxon *cyning*, denoting ability, skill, or knowledge, which in turn is cognate with German verb *können* (to be able) and the related word *kennen* (to know). Thus, ideally the king is the one who is most able to lead and who knows what is best for the well-being of his tribe.

In an interesting article, published in 2023 in the magazine *New Dawn*, John Michael Greer writes that in the Celtic and Germanic parts of Europe the king was regarded as being wedded to the land.[1] It was the land itself, typically portrayed as a goddess, that gave him his authority. In certain cases his queen functioned as the representative of the goddess. The installation of the king was carried out in a place sacred to the tribe and was attended by various ritual practices and tests of the candidate's worth. Greer mentions that the kings of Tara had to step on a sacred stone, which was said to shout for joy when it recognized the foot of the rightful king. Something similar is described in the Arthurian legends when the future king, Arthur, pulls the sword Excalibur from a stone.

Such traditions became eroded with the Christianization of Europe when the church took over the function of anointing and crowning monarchs, but Greer points out that the British monarchy has retained its ancient coronation ritual, the only royal house in Europe to do so. British kings and queens are still crowned according to a procedure set out in the *Liber Regalis* (Royal Book), dating from 1308, which contains certain of the old pre-Christian elements. All of this helps to create an emotional bond between the people and the monarch and to foster in the population a sense of shared history and tradition. That is why I hope the pillar of the monarchy will be preserved.

21

Excursions into Enchantment

About twenty minutes' drive from our house is the small, picturesque town of Worpswede, lying amid the moorlands of Lower Saxony. At the end of the nineteenth century it gave birth to a famous school of landscape painting as well as to a short-lived utopian commune. The poet Rilke was one of those who frequented the place in its heyday. The town is still an artistic center with many galleries as well as the studios of painters, sculptors, and craftspeople of various kinds. With three of its residents I came to have valued friendships.

One of them I first met in the summer of 2019, when the studios of Worpswede were holding an open day. On the Worpswede website I found a list of the participating artists, and something told me to go first of all to the studio of a sculptor called Ulrich Conrad, although I had not heard of him. On the drive to Worpswede I nourished the hope that Conrad would not be typical of the modern arts world, which I generally dislike for its betrayal of beauty, its rejection of tradition, and its sycophantic courtiers who go on kowtowing to a naked emperor.

On the road where he lived I parked the car on a grassy verge and walked up a driveway leading to the property: a small white house and various outbuildings surrounding a grassy area with some trees, where I could already glimpse some of the sculptures as well as the sculptor himself—a tall, elderly man with a patrician bearing and a distinguished aquiline profile. He was standing talking to three other visitors, a man and two women, and he invited me to join the group.

Leading us to an exquisite little bronze sculpture of a young man on a horse, he told us that he had always had a special love of horses and over the years had assembled a large collection of bridles and horse bits. The two women drifted away, leaving me and the other visitor, a painter. We moved on to a small bronze figure of a man playing a lute.

"The Germans used to be a nation of singers," Conrad said wistfully, "until the end of war. Now some sing again, but not to the same extent as before." He rejected the modernist insistence on abstraction, and the painter agreed, saying that the galleries always lost interest in his work when they found out that it was representational. The more Conrad talked, the clearer it became that he was deeply disaffected with the prevailing German establishment and indignant at what he saw as the systematic brainwashing of the Germans to purge them of any sense of national pride. It became clear that he was a man with conservative views but decidedly no Nazi.

He led us on to a lovely sculpture of a naked woman, tenderly clasping a baby to her breast. He explained that the theme of motherhood was a particularly emotional one for him, as his own mother had died of tuberculosis about two years after his birth. Beside one of the outbuildings was the monument that had once marked her grave: a wooden cross with a wreath of roses and some loving words. It might have been the grave of an older, more gracious Germany that had vanished . . . but perhaps not quite, for a few remnants of it could still be found, and I felt that Ulrich Conrad's domain was one of them. He showed us more sculptures: a man standing in front of a prancing horse, a pair of hands loosely clasped as though protecting some tender thing like a butterfly. I thought how just one of his sculptures was worth all of the meaningless, depressing works of art that are publicly displayed in Bremen, as in cities all over the world.

Before I left he invited me to come again, and on a subsequent visit I met his partner Elke and we talked over tea and cakes in their house. On another occasion he drove over to Lilienthal to see my sculptures, which he praised. About an hour after leaving, he returned bringing me a special kind of hammer for my woodcarving. I felt honored. Since then I have visited Ulrich and Elke many times and have come to regard them as much valued friends.

Another resident of Worpswede whom I got to know was the geomancer Harald Jordan—sadly only for a short time, as he died about a year and a half after I was introduced to him in March 2022 by our mutual friend Reinhard Wolff. Earlier in life he had been a very successful engineer with an expensive lifestyle. Then, as a result of a personal crisis, he radically reexamined his life during a period of retreat in the Tyrol and began to study and practice geomancy and dowsing, eventually establishing himself as a teacher and writer in these areas.

He met us in front of the old half-timbered former farm building where he lived on the edge of Worpswede, a handsome, elderly man looking strikingly like a North American Indian chief, with hatchet-like features and white hair drawn back into a ponytail. The house was friendly in a minimalistic sort of way, with a book-lined entrance hall doubling as a study, and a rather bare living room with an old tree trunk in the middle, surrounded by a circle of stones. We had a very convivial conversation over coffee and cake, and I showed him pictures of my garden sculptures. Before I left he gave me two of his publications: a booklet on Worpswede and a book entitled *Räume der Kraft schaffen* (*Creating Spaces of Power*). These are inspiring works that explore the relationship between ourselves, our environment, nature, and the cosmos, and describe how we can work to optimize that relationship. On a later occasion I visited him together with my Norwegian friend Harald Harklau, and he showed us a kind of monochord instrument called an elikon, with which one can demonstrate Pythagorean intervals in music.

Meanwhile I continued to develop my own kind of sacred space. From the stonemason Frank Graupner I had acquired an old gravestone with a rose carved into it. I added a line from Théophile Gautier's poem "Spectre de la Rose": "*Çi gît une rose que tous les rois vont jalouser*" (Here lies a rose that all kings will envy). Against a wall opposite the stone I placed a wrought-iron bench with a rose pattern, a gift from Donate. I remember years ago in London seeing the ballet *Spectre de la Rose*, based on Gautier's poem, with choreography by Michel Fokine and music by Carl Maria von Weber, featuring the Russian dancer Rudolf Nureyev. So now I could sit on the bench and hear the ballet music in my mind. I also made a stele dedicated to Hermann Löns, the poet of the Lüneburg Heath, with some lines written by him:

> "*Wandle still, so werden dir*
> *Geheime Dinge kund.*"

(Wander in silence, and secret things will be made known to you.)

It was now the autumn of 2022—an eventful and often troubled year. The Covid epidemic was still continuing, and both Donate and I came down with it, although in a fairly mild form, both of us having been vaccinated four times. International news was often far from cheerful, with the war in the Ukraine still raging. In August came the death of Mikhail Gorbachev, whom I had once heard give a speech in Hamburg and been very impressed by. He had worked hard to achieve détente with the West and almost succeeded. The outbreak of a new Russophobia and the conflict in Ukraine must have saddened him greatly. Just over a week after his death came that of the Queen, which I have spoken of earlier.

In our private lives there were many happy events. Donate's numerous relatives had established the tradition of having a big family reunion every couple of years, and the one for 2022 was held in May at a youth hostel in Possenhofen on the shore of Lake Starnberg in Bavaria, territory that was very familiar to me from the researches for my biography of King Ludwig II of Bavaria. Possenhofen Castle was where Ludwig's cousin Elisabeth ("Sissi"), later empress of Austria, grew up. Part of the local railway station had been turned into a museum devoted to her memory. And in the lake, a short boat ride away, was the Roseninsel (Rose Island), which was one of Ludwig's favorite retreats and where we spent a delightful morning. In July Donate went for a three-week health cure to Überlingen on Lake Constance, and I joined her there for part of the time.

In November I went to England to visit family and attend another meeting of our Anonymous Society. Traveling by bus through central London I experienced how much the city has changed since I lived there, and generally not for the better. It was as though someone had decided to make London look more like New York by plonking hideous high-rise buildings on every available site without any regard to harmony. Everywhere there were trendy new restaurants, expensive-looking shops, and garish advertisements. The streets were impossibly crowded, and the noise level was intense—every so often an ambulance or a police car would go past with siren blaring. On the surface there was an atmosphere of brash commercialism, but one had the feeling that it was all an attempt to divert attention from the serious problems of the country, such as poverty and homelessness—both evident in London with beggars and people sleeping on the streets.

From London I took a bus to Oxford. That year the Anonymous Society had an afternoon meeting in Christ Church, a nostalgic experience for us. Afterward we dined in the Great Hall. We then relaxed and chatted in the cozy senior common room. After a hearty breakfast the next morning I set off by bus to visit my son Jason and his family in Tring. The bus went through glorious countryside, past woods and hedgerows bright with autumn colors and through old, picture-postcard villages. The journey reassured me that there was still life in the old England that I remembered.

22

Celebrating My First Eighty Years

I draw this memoir to a close in my eighty-first year. As I look back, I have much to be grateful for. I have been privileged to live for most of my life in comparatively safe and stable countries. I have had a many-faceted and exciting career, while still having time to write books and pursue a life of the mind and a fulfilling spiritual quest. I have been blessed by a wonderful family, dear loved ones, and many friends. A number of people have been kind enough to say that I have inspired them. If so, I feel honored.

I am writing this chapter in the summer of 2024, and tragically the world scene is full of turmoil. Despite the devastating war in Ukraine *Occult Russia* came out in December 2022, and early the following year, on top of various podcast interviews, I made another lecture trip to California to speak at the Scottish Rite about the Russia book and at Templum Rosae Lodge about my forthcoming work *Occult Germany*. Again I received kind hospitality from my California brethren, who put me up in Berkeley in the wonderful Berkeley City Club, built in the 1920s by the architect Julia Morgan, an extraordinary woman who was the first of her sex to study architecture at the École de Beaux Arts in Paris and the first to qualify as an architect in California. The building was a sheer delight to be in, reminiscent of an Italian palazzo and filled with beautiful decorative detail and works of art, carefully chosen by the architect. There were lots of cozy, softly lit corners, two loggias with plants, a swimming pool, and a library with many interesting books. During the visit my California brethren were generous with their time. I was taken by Adam Kendall on a marvelous tour around the San Francisco Bay area, and by Jonathan Prestage around the California Grand Lodge building in San Francisco.

Back home, work on my sculptures continued. From a stone merchant I bought a slab of fine gold-colored sandstone, paid for as an advance birthday present from my brother, David. I carved into it a low relief incorporating the Yggdrasil, Odin's two ravens, and other motifs from the *Edda*. Working on the stone put me in mind of a passage that I remembered reading in a book by Martin Buber called *The Way of Man* about the teachings of the Hasidic sage, the Baal-Shem. I went to my bookshelves and found the book and the passage:

"The Baal-Shem teaches that no encounter with a being or a thing in the course of our life lacks a hidden significance. The people we live with or meet . . . the materials we shape, the tools we use, they all contain a mysterious spiritual substance which depends on us for helping it towards its pure form, its perfection."[1]

If artists, architects, and all who shape our physical environment were to work in this spirit, then we would be living in a much more beautiful world.

In June 2023 came another Esoteric Quest conference organized by Ralph White, this time to Tomar in Portugal on the theme of the Knights Templar, who survived in Portugal under the name of the Knights of Christ after they were suppressed elsewhere in the early fourteenth century. I flew to Lisbon and took a taxi to the Airbnb lodging that I had booked in the Rua dos Cavaleiros, a steep, narrow street of old houses, full of little shops and cafés. Unfortunately the Feast of St. Anthony was in progress. Up and down the street people were partying, playing music, shouting, and singing. The noise was deafening, and I got very little sleep. Next morning I joined the Esoteric Quest group at another hotel, and we went by bus to the Hotel dos Templarios in Tomar, a beautiful old town that was once a great center of the Templars, a fact of which the city was obviously proud, as there were Templar souvenirs everywhere: statuettes, mugs, plates, and ornaments of all kinds. Among our group were many old friends from previous Esoteric Quests, including Joscelyn Godwin, Paul Bembridge, Leonard George, Marjorie Roth, and the Quest team of Ralph White, Carrie Wykoff, and Andrea Lomanto.

There has long been a debate among historians as to whether the Templars were guardians of some esoteric teaching or were simply a pious order of warrior monks dedicated to defending the Christian faith and the church. It became clear during the course of the conference that the weight of evidence is in favor of the former view. The Portuguese writer Nuno Ferreira Goncalves, for example, gave a fascinating talk linking the Templars with the Grail mystery, the Brethren of Purity, the Sufis, and the sect of the Assassins. I gave a general overview of the history of the Templars as well as a talk on neo-Templarism. And there were talks about more general aspects of Portuguese culture, such as the work of the artist Lima de Freitas, which Joscelyn Godwin spoke about. We were given a tour of Tomar's Hermetic Museum and a dinner in the castle overlooking the town, accompanied by a performance of Fado music. It was altogether a rich program.

Soon after I returned home Joscelyn Godwin came to Lilienthal for five nights, and Aaron French also joined us for a few days. We drove over to Worpswede, walked in the footsteps of the poet Rainer Maria Rilke and the painter and revolutionary Heinrich Vogeler, and conversed for an hour or so over coffee and cakes in one of the delightful cafés of the town. We also spent much time at the McIntosh home in Lilienthal, where I gave Joscelyn and Aaron a conducted tour of the Garden of the Mysteries, showing them the sundial of the four elements, the runic circle, the steles to Orpheus, Pan, and Apollo, and the other features. A corner of the terrace, surrounded by such things, was an ideal setting in which to sit and talk. We did not, as I recall, talk much about our respective books and researches. Among such kindred spirits there is a kind of rapport that is palpable even when the talk is of "shoes and ships and sealing wax and cabbages and kings" and of a thousand little everyday things.

Two months later came sad news. Nobuko Somers called me one morning to say that Jeffrey had died of a heart attack. He had been ill for some time and had needed full-time care. I lit a candle for him. He had been a very kind and supportive friend to me, as had Nobuko after their marriage, and I regretted not having seen more of them after I left England.

Autumn came and marked a special anniversary. By then Donate and I had been together for twenty years since that coffee break in the Hamburg Museum of Ethnology in 2003. Thursday, September 21 was my eightieth birthday. The main celebration was to be on Sunday, but meanwhile we celebrated quietly at home with a birthday breakfast, and Donate gave me her presents: two beautiful sweaters, a big box of English tea, and two jars of English marmalade. Over the next couple of days various birthday guests arrived, including my sister, June, and brother-in-law, Terry, from Pennsylvania. On Saturday evening we had a pre-party get-together in a Chinese restaurant, and the following day

Fig. 22.1. A musical interlude at my eightieth birthday party in
September 2023. The players are (*left to right*) Donate McIntosh
(*drum*), my brother David (*banjo*), my sister June (*spoons*), and
yours truly (*guitar and vocal*).

a big breakfast-cum-lunch in a private room at a restaurant near
our house, with twenty-one people present. Halfway through the
meal we had a break for entertainment, starting with a rendering
of the Cockney song "Knocked 'em in the Old Kent Road," sung
by me with Donate playing a drum, June on the wooden spoons,
and David and me with our guitars. David then sang a song that he
had composed in my honor, Donate gave a hilarious rendering of
Goethe's poem "Erlkönig" with phonetic punctuation, and Angus
and Jason recited the following poem about me:

A poem to celebrate the eightieth birthday of
Christopher McIntosh

*Composed by Katja Haars, ChatGPT,
and Angus McIntosh*

In northern lands where legends blend with snow
Lives Christopher McIntosh, his passions aglow,
A heart that dances with myths of ages past,
And Plattdeutsch in his soul, a love so vast.
He speaks in tongues of ancient German lore,
With every word, the spirits to implore,
His language whispers secrets of the earth,
Connecting him to legends and their worth.
In runes and sagas he finds his delight,
Norse gods and heroes in the moon's soft light.
Thor's thunder echoes in his beating heart,
As Christopher unravels myths in art.
He dreams of Yggdrasil, the world ash tree,
Its roots and branches, life's tapestry.
As guardian of knowledge does he stand,
A scholar yet with Mjölnir in hand
With each Plattdeutsch phrase a rune comes alive,
A bridge between the realms where legends thrive,
Christopher McIntosh, a northern sage,
In myth and language, finds his endless page.
In the lore of the North he finds his muse,
As Norse sagas and legends he does peruse,
From Odin's wisdom to Thor's hammer blow,
Always entranced by the northern light's glow.
But amidst these myths and realms so high
Here stands Donate, forever nigh.
Together they journey through life's terrain,

As stars in a mythic, celestial domain,
Through Yggdrasil's branches their spirits soar,
As together they find what they both adore.
In the fields of myth their story is sown,
And happiness and love, their crop, has grown.

I can think of no better note on which to end this account of the first eight decades of my life's journey.

Fig. 22.2. My sons, Jason (*left*) and Angus,
reading a poem in my honor at my eightieth birthday.

Notes

Chapter 1.
A Hermetic Baptism

1. Louis Effingham de Forest, *Ancestry of William Seaman Bainbrdge* (Oxford: The Scrivener Press, 1950), 124.

Chapter 2.
Magic and Mystery in
Oxford and London

1. The Master Therion (Aleister Crowley), *Magic in Theory and Practice* (Paris: Lecram Press, 1929), vii.
2. Dion Fortune, *The Winged Bull* (London: Aquarian Press, 1971), 9.

Chapter 5.
Second Marriage and
Oxford Revisited

1. William Morris, *News from Nowhere* (London: Longmans Green, 1907), 51.

Chapter 7.
Experiencing Sacred Space

1. David A. Mason, *Spirit of the Mountains: Korea's SAN-SHIN and Traditions of Mountain-Worship* (Elizabeth, New Jersey, and Seoul, Korea: Hollym, 1999).

Chapter 8.
Key Encounters

1. "Seemann, wo ist deine Heimat?," music by Karl Götz, words by Heinz Schuhmacher, first released in 1954.
2. Frederic Lamond, *Religion without Beliefs* (London: Janus Publishing Company, 1997), 46.
3. Lamond, *Religion without Beliefs*, 46.
4. Lamond, *Religion without Beliefs*, 47.

Chapter 9.
The Gods on Forty-Second Street

1. The first of two lectures by Hillman in the series *Mythic Journeys*, organized by Mythic Imagination, an institute devoted to exploring the accumulated wisdom inherent in stories, myths, and legends. The Hillman lectures are posted on YouTube.
2. James Hillman, "Many Gods, Many Persons," in James Hillman, *A Blue Fire* (New York: Harper Perennial, 1991), 39.
3. James Hillman, *Revisioning Psychology* (New York: Harper Perennial, 1992).
4. Hillman, *Revisioning Psychology*, 2–3.
5. Arthur Versluis, *Entering the Mysteries: The Secret Traditions of Indigenous Europe* (Minneapolis, Minnesota: New Culture Press, 2016), 12.
6. Christopher McIntosh, *Master of the Starlit Grove and Other Stories* (Bremen, Germany: Vanadis Texts, 2014).
7. Dion Fortune, *The Goat-Foot God* (London: Aquarian Press, 1971), epigraph on unnumbered pre-title page.
8. Fortune, *The Goat-Foot God*, 352–53.
9. Gerald B. Gardner, *Witchcraft Today* (London: Arrow Books, 1970), 47.
10. Robert Graves, *The White Goddess* (London: Faber and Faber, 1959), 476–77.
11. Hans Thomas Hakl, *Eranos: An Alternative Intellectual History of the Twentieth Century* (Sheffield, UK: Equinox, 2013).
12. David Miller, *The New Polytheism: Rebirth of the Gods and Goddesses* (Thompson, Connecticut: Spring Publications, 2021).
13. Alain de Benoist, *On Being a Pagan*, English translation (Atlanta, Georgia: Ultra, 2004), electronic version, 6–7.
14. De Benoist, *On Being a Pagan*, 16.

Chapter 12.
Books, Travels, and Crises

1. Hans Thomas Hakl, *Eranos: An Alternative Intellectual History of the Twentieth Century* (Sheffield, UK: Equinox, 2013), 2.

Chapter 13.
Aspects of Mercury and Odin

1. Joscelyn Godwin, Christopher McIntosh, and Donate Pahnke McIntosh, *Rosicrucian Trilogy* (Newburyport, Massachusetts: Weiser Books, 2016).
2. Hans Thomas Hakl (ed.), Octagon (Gaggenau, Germany: Scientia Nova, 2015–2018). Essays celebrating Dr. Hakl's esoteric library, 4 volumes (German, English, Italian, French).
3. Robert Graves, *The White Goddess*, 9–10.

Chapter 20.
The Rose Cross and the Internet

1. John Michael Greer, "The Crown and Ancient Rites of Kingship," *New Dawn*, no. 199, July–August 2023, 57–61.

Chapter 22.
Celebrating My First Eighty Years

1. Martin Buber, *The Way of Man* (Secaucus, N.J.: Citadel Press, 1966), 38.

Index

Page numbers in *italics* indicate illustrations

Laban, Rudolf, 147
Laima, 179
Lammas festival, 172–73
Lamond, Frederic, 110–12, 120
Langeoog, 161–62
Langhus, 143, 167
Langhus Folk Dance Group, 145–46, *pl. 8*
Latvia conference, 178–79
Laxminarayan Temple, 95
Leaves of Yggdrasil (Aswynn), 50, 71
Lebensborn Spy, The, 158, 171
Lebensborn Boy, The, 155–56
"Legacy of Nordic and Teutonic Mythology, The," 195
legends and fairy tales, 14–15
Lévi, Eliphas, 23, 31–32
Lews Castle conference, 201–2
Librairie Vega, 33
Lilienthal, 183, 203, 223, 229–30. *See also* Garden of Mysteries
Lindblad Polaris, 63–64
Lithuania, 179–80
Little Sparta, 42–43, 200, 202
Loewe, Eva, 59
Loki, 2
London
  1984 temporary accommodations, 64
  Addison Road flat, 58–59
  Bloomsbury, 30–32
  esoteric bookshops, 32–33
  as esoteric crossroads, 34
  esoteric events, 34–35
  esoteric figures, 27–29
  experience of, 25–27
  farewell dinner, 79–80

  first job, 25
  Highbury flat, 64, 70
  Holland Park flat, 63
  libraries, 26–27
  music scene, 35
  publishing, 35–36
Long Night of the Religions, 195–96
Lost World of the Kalahari, The, (van der Post), 87–88
Louisenlund park, 101
Low German (Plattdeutsch), 144–45
Ludwig project, 210
Luhrmann, Tanya, 49–50, 51
Lumb, David, 169

maenad relief (Garden of Mysteries), 189, 190, *pl. 14*
magic
  in achieving an ideal, 53
  approach to, 53
  ceremonial, 49
  demonic, 36
  Gerald Yorke and, 40
  ritual, 29, 31, 50–53, 219
  seidh, 180
  wands, 28–29, 33
  world, opening of, 26
Magick in Theory and Practice (Crowley), 23
Man, Myth and Magic, 35
Mara, 179
marriage. *See* Donate•(wife); Katherine (wife)
Master of the Starlit Grove (McIntosh), 171
Matthews, John, 108